Praise for *The Murder of Innocence*

"*The Murder of Innocence* tells the true story of a young man destroyed by mental illness, brought about by repeated sexual abuse at the hands of his parish priest. We witness Michael's story unfold in heartbreaking detail through a patchwork of first-person family narratives, childhood photographs, medical records, memos, and legal documents. Through it all is woven the loving honesty of his younger brother, Sam, as he fights with the continued betrayal of his brother by the Catholic Church. It is also a work of courage and an attempt at justice and healing. Read it; you won't soon forget it."

— Donald R. Ross, MD; Clinical Associate Professor, Psychiatry, University of Maryland School of Medicine and retired from Sheppard Pratt Hospital, #6 in Psychiatry in the U.S.

"This is an incredibly powerful book. I can't tell if it is sadness or fury that has tears falling down my face, but I want to hear the whole story—and then do something!"

— Cheri Lennie, philanthropist and child advocate

"There is not a day that goes by that I don't think of Michael—whether it's his sense of humor, his loud infectious laugh, his ability to listen and give caring, attentive advice, or his eagerness to learn and try new things. Michael was my soulmate and best friend. I am so grateful that I had the honor of having him in my life. His tragic death completely shifted my universe. Sadly, Michael's story is too common—the hidden pain and secrets that took over his life due to his being sexually abused as a child. *The Murder of Innocence: The Truth about Sexual Abuse and the Catholic Church* finally tells his story and frees the hidden pain that so many secretly cope with."

— Alli Schwartz, Entrepreneur and Founder, GFit Women; a *Main Line Today* 2017 Woman on the Move

"This book is a dedication to lives lost due to the betrayal of trust under the guise of religious love. Michael's passing is a visceral reminder of how vulnerable we are to those who maliciously use their power of influence, cloaked as messengers of a higher being, to commit ungodly sins. I highly recommend reading this important and tragic story."

— Mac M. Martirossian, Founder and Managing Director,
MThree Advisory Services, LLC

"The Best Book I've Read Thus Far in 2019. This is a nonfiction book, and it's not for the faint-hearted."

— Frank W. Kresen, Copy Editor and Proofreader,
proof positive, Kansas City, Missouri

"With a keen and analytical mind, author Sam Unglo with his new book, *The Murder of Innocence,* deftly expresses the pain, torment, and heartbreak experienced by innocent victims of pedophiles from the Catholic Clergy and child sex abuse's lasting impact on victims' family and friends. Unglo sharply pierces the veil of theocracy's stranglehold on innocent lives while delivering a potent warning that pedophilia shall no longer be tolerated. *The Murder of Innocence* really comprises the murder of a human soul. Michael's story fully supports why child sex abuse victims' rights to justice in a court of law should be timeless—that there should be no statute of limitations—as child sex abuse is murder—the murder of innocence."

— Howard R. Osofsky, Esq.
J.D., Emory University School of Law
Founding Partner, Bexley & Osofsky, P.C.

"I beg you to have patience with everything unresolved in your heart and to try to love the questions themselves as if they were locked rooms or books written in a very foreign language. Don't search for the answers, which could not be given to you now, because you would not be able to live them. And the point is to live everything. Live the questions now. Perhaps then, someday far in the future, you will gradually, without even noticing it, live your way into the answer."

— Rainer Maria Rilke,
Letters to a Young Poet, 1929

Michael had a knack for sending family and friends inspirational cards. The above was on the front of a card he sent me on November 27, 2004, a few weeks after he and I had completed the New York City Marathon together on November 7, 2004. Inside, he wrote:

> "I couldn't pass up this card, since the author Rilke is one of our cousin Ralph's favorites to quote. In fact, Ralph had me read from Rilke the last time I was at his house in August.
> "Thank you for taking care of our photo order. The memory of us crossing arm-in-arm is one I'll always hold dear to my heart.
> "— Love, Michael"

At the time, I didn't know how much I would come to cherish this card and our marathon together in New York—and how true the words on the front are.

THE **TRUTH** ABOUT **SEXUAL ABUSE**
AND THE **CATHOLIC CHURCH**

THE MURDER OF INNOCENCE

SAM UNGLO

Copyrighted Material

The Murder of Innocence: The Truth about Sexual Abuse and the Catholic Church.

Copyright © 2019 by Just Be Publishing Co. All Rights Reserved.

No part of this publication may be reproduced, stored in a retrieval system or transmitted, in any form or by any means—electronic, mechanical, photocopying, recording or otherwise—without prior written permission from the publisher, except for the inclusion of brief quotations in a review.

For information about this title or to order other books or electronic media, please write to info@justbepublishingco.com at Just Be Publishing Co.

Library of Congress Control Number: 2019910442

ISBN: 978-1-7332453-0-2 (Hardcover)
978-1-7332453-1-9 (Softcover)
978-1-7332453-2-6 (eBook)

Printed in the United States of America

Cover and Interior design: 1106 Design

Publisher's Cataloging-In-Publication Data
(Prepared by The Donohue Group, Inc.)

Names: Unglo, Sam, 1975- author. | Unglo, Michael R., 1971-2010, author.
Title: The murder of innocence : the truth about sexual abuse and the Catholic Church / Sam Unglo.
Description: [Roswell, Georgia] : Just Be Publishing Co., [2019] | Contains "… Michael's unedited and uncensored writings."--page 5.
Identifiers: ISBN 9781733245302 (hardcover) | ISBN 9781733245319 (softcover) | ISBN 9781733245326 (ebook)
Subjects: LCSH: Unglo, Michael R., 1971-2010. | Unglo, Sam, 1975---Family. | Child sexual abuse by clergy--United States. | Adult child sexual abuse victims--United States--Biography. | Child sexual abuse--Religious aspects--Catholic Church. | Sexual abuse victims--Family relationships. | Catholic Church--Clergy--Sexual behavior. | LCGFT: Biographies.
Classification: LCC RC569.5.A28 U54 2019 (print) | LCC RC569.5.A28 (ebook) | DDC 616.858369--dc23

Preface: Ready to Publish

I have wanted to publish a book to honor my brother, Michael Unglo, ever since he died on May 4, 2010, a day that I will never forget.

I received a call from Austen Riggs, a mental-healthcare facility in Stockbridge, Massachusetts, where Michael was receiving care. I was in my office at work staring out the window as I answered, "This is Sam Unglo."

The attending physician said, "Michael is gone."

I knew what *gone* meant as I heard a nurse wailing in the background. Michael was dead.

Michael often said that he was working on writing a book. A common refrain in the family was, "When are you going to publish your book, Michael? What is it about?" My mom would especially ask that last question, as she thought there was something damning in the book about her. Michael never saw his book through, though. That would come to fall on my shoulders as he shared his writings with me, which are a part of this book—his unedited and uncensored writings. Sharing those will answer the second question.

It has been almost a decade since Michael died. Holding myself accountable, I have often said to myself, "Why is it taking so long? Hurry the hell up!" The short answer is that the process has been complex. A slightly longer answer is that Michael's death was tragic and that I had my own work to do to achieve a state of mindfulness and balance where I could best publish a work for him, inclusive of more material other than his own writings, to tell his story and, to some extent, mine.

I am self-publishing. I had visions of landing a literary agent and getting a major publisher. I failed at both—many times. My dreams of having help with a national book tour were dashed—at least for now. At this point, though, that is their loss, and to some extent, I am glad that I failed so much. For a while, I worked with a ghostwriter whose focus was on business books. While he was helpful in many ways, for which I am grateful, he thought that the book needed a how-to element to make a tragic story more publishable. That really was not what Michael wanted, though.

The memoir and biography approaches are more of what Michael wanted. I also pitched those approaches to literary agents and publishers, and I was greeted with the following feedback: "You've never published before. You don't have a platform. What makes you an expert? Who is your audience? Why would someone want to read this book?"

I have accomplished many firsts in my life for my family and me, and this is simply another one of those. I feel accomplished and qualified enough. I graduated with honors from both Cornell University (Bachelor of Science) and Georgia State University (Master of Business Administration). Professionally, I am the chief financial officer for the leading youth-development nonprofit in the United States, Boys & Girls Clubs of America. So, I am not exactly unqualified and a dunce. I am a first-time book author, though.

In terms of my audience, broadly, it is anyone who will listen and who wants to bring about positive change. The people who I most want to read the book are pedophiles—because they need to understand the horrendous damage they cause, and they need to stop and get help before destroying someone else's innocence. Of course, they likely will not read the book. That leaves my family, friends, and others wanting to know how a truly beautiful person's innocence was

Preface: Ready to Publish

destroyed by abuses of power and by a pedophile. We can all take steps to combat the factors that went into killing Michael.

More specific audiences might include the following if you identify better with any of these: victims of child sex abuse, victims' loved ones, leaders in the catholic church (more on refusing to capitalize these two words later), churchgoers and society in general, lawmakers, and my own children.

The victims of child sex abuse. This book helps to document the pain and torment you have suffered. The situation in which Michael was put is an example of the burden you are forced to carry starting at such a young age. Innocence is shattered so violently, and often times, you do not come forward or tell anyone until you are older and people start to view you as an adult. Other adults start to blame you, and you even start to blame yourself, and both of those blames are misdirected.

Victims' loved ones. Parents, siblings, significant others, and friends need to know the best way to respond and can learn from Michael's life. I explore and present my own learning from having gone through this ordeal. There are ways in which I would have acted differently. We can all learn from what happened to my brother, including me.

Leaders in the catholic church or other institutions in which child sex abuse has taken place. The pope and bishops in the church respond on their own terms, continue to support ex-priests financially, and fail to give the victims what they need. To the pope directly, I hope you read this book. I would love to have a conversation with you someday that leads to the action I recommend, not the action that you think you can infallibly recommend. There is no such thing as papal infallibility. Last I checked, you are a human, and all humans make mistakes. It is how they correct them that matters, and you and your bishops have not corrected yours on the subject of child sex abuse.

Churchgoers and society in general. You should not sit on the sidelines and be passive. You also need to be an active voice in how you act and what you demand. You should not be an innocent bystander who does nothing. When you do nothing, you only support the lack of an adequate response by leaders such as the pope, who have their own interests to protect. By learning and understanding from this book, you should be better equipped to act to bring about positive change. Don't be silent.

Lawmakers. Some states have lifted the statute of limitations (e.g., two years) on child sex abuse. All states need to lift the statute of limitations so that victims can come forth at any time in their life to bring justice. The two-year or any other time limitation does not make sense for young victims, who cannot process everything until much later on than two years from the last incident of abuse. Child sex abuse is akin to murder. It is the murder of innocence. There should not be any statute of limitations.

My own children. I want them to know Uncle Michael's full story and to be proud of their uncle. As well, I want them to learn from our family's history so that they do not repeat some of the same mistakes in their own lives and with their children. When we truly know and understand, we stand a much better chance of not repeating history. We act deliberately and consciously with knowledge, wisdom, and understanding. While I have broken many unhealthy cycles myself, they will likely still have a few to break themselves or to keep broken (e.g., that they do not errantly choose catholicism or any other religion without knowing Michael's true story).

That beautiful person, Michael, who had his innocence destroyed, had many lasting positive contributions to this world and impacted my life profoundly and positively. Readers of this book will also learn of some of his brilliance and loving ways, and maybe incorporate those into their own lives, further carrying on his legacy.

Preface: Ready to Publish

One recent piece of advice I received was, "What is the point of your book?" My book's main point is to honor Michael's wish for a book that would serve as a reference point for his life well after he and I are gone—no other accounts to rely on altered by time or memories that do not adequately portray his own writings and feelings and might distort what really happened. Too often, in my family and in others I have seen, tragedies or family secrets are swept under the carpet or distorted if they are passed down verbally from one generation to the next. For example, already, my mom likes to say that Michael "got sick" the past couple years of his life. The reality is that his struggle started when the abuse started. He was the victim of a religious culture that taught blind obedience to religious authorities who were supposedly infallible—the pope chief among them. Michael himself was a great man who accomplished an astonishing amount for any man, let alone someone in his circumstances. This book will be on the shelf forever for those who want to know my brother's true story. A summary statement such as, "He got sick," or, "He committed suicide," does not adequately testify to his life's work. I am proud of my brother and of his story. I hope you learn from it as I have. In short, he wanted, and I want, truth to be preserved.

There are other hopes for and points of the book, but that is the main one. Perhaps, in reading it, you will find a point or points of the book all for yourself. I hope you do.

One of Michael's passions was lifelong learning. Here's to your own continued learning.

> *"We can lift ourselves out of ignorance, we can find ourselves as creatures of excellence and intelligence and skill. We can be free! We can learn to fly!"*
> — Richard Bach, *Jonathan Livingston Seagull*

Contents

Part One: Michael 1
    1. Innocence Shattered 3
    2. Pretty Traumatic Love—Michael, Autumn 2008 5
    3. Meaningful Survival—Michael, January 2009 17
    4. Trauma—Michael, July 2009 33

Part Two: More Than Just Bad Church Leadership 37
    5. Michael's Suicide and My Introductory Thoughts 39
    6. Timeline 43
    7. The First Time Michael Tried to Tell, My Mom's Complexities, and Family Dynamics 49
    8. Dorsch's Attempt on Our Oldest Brother, Paul—but No One Takes Heed 59

Part Three: The Battle with the catholic church 61
    9. Why catholic-Related Words Appear in Lowercase: Beware of Authority 63
    10. The Perpetrator: Richard J. Dorsch 77
    11. Correspondence with the diocese of Pittsburgh RE: Support of and for Michael 89
    12. Lawsuit Filed 117

Part Four: More on Michael and Me 125

13. No Turning Back 127
14. Changing Your Paradigm about Loved Ones 131
15. Homelessness 135
16. Michael's Shame and Fallout from Being Sexually Abused Ages 10–14 by a Priest 141

Part Five: Grieving and Evolving 159

17. My Grieving Process 161
18. Breaking My Own Silence 187
19. My Sister Frances's Thoughts on Our Dad, the church, and Michael 195
20. What I Would Have Done Differently 215

Part Six: Loose Ends 219

21. For the Common Good 221
22. What Survivors of Child Sex Abuse Want 223
23. It's Worth Living 227
24. Letter to Michael 231
25. Resources 237
26. Some of Michael's Other Writings 241
27. Closing Thoughts 249

About the Author 255

Part One

Michael

1

Innocence Shattered

The following is an excerpt from the letter Michael wrote (dated July 20, 2008) to the diocese of Pittsburgh after his first suicide attempt in 2008 (the night of Friday, June 20, 2008). He was asked to write the letter by the diocese to document why he was seeking assistance from them as he continued to heal from his suicide attempt and the underlying complex post-traumatic stress disorder (C-PTSD) that was a direct result of the sex abuse he suffered as a child at the hands of Richard Dorsch, then a priest employed by the diocese, in the early 1980s.

> . . . My abuser, Richard Dorsch, violated my family's trust in him. After my dad passed away, my mom was led by Dorsch to believe it was okay for her to let him take me on day trips. One occasion stands out due to the violent intensity of the abuse—sexual, physical, and emotional. Dorsch led me to a trail—then known as 'The Braille Trail'—saying he wanted to teach me how blind people read. The incident replayed itself and resulted in my attempt to take my own life the night of Friday, 20 June 2008. That day on the trail back in 1983, Dorsch had me close my eyes. He guided my hand across

a Braille sign. Then, his hand squeezed tight on mine. He forcibly restrained me.

I said, "Father, that hurts!"

He said, "It's going to be okay," as he gripped my hand around his penis.

I cried out through tears, "No, Father!"

His grip got tighter, and he kept his hand clasped around mine as he forced me to masturbate him to ejaculate. I was sobbing. I felt humiliated, ashamed, and violated. He said that this is what made our love special and that only he and I were to know.

He always said that, as if to threaten me. I was paralyzed emotionally . . .

2

Pretty Traumatic Love— Michael, Autumn 2008

(This chapter and the next two are Michael's unedited and uncensored writings as he shared with me. I am George. Those who know our family can piece together the rest.)

This story is dedicated to all survivors. Thanks to mom's multitudinous love, Gina's wit, Jake's hands, Barbara's pointers, and George's indefatigability! Names of people have been changed to mask identity in an effort, however bound to ineptitude, to protect privacy. Thanks, above all, to my dad, who sacrificed his all for every one of us!

Any similarities to or differences from actual events are by-products of long-term memory impairment that is a symptom of my complex post-traumatic stress disorder, a psychiatric condition for which I continue to receive counseling by a specialized therapist and take fluoxetine (i.e., generic Prozac—it's cheaper) every morning with or without coffee.

The Murder of Innocence

Wee Hours of Sunday, March 22, 1981
The day began not unlike so many others at the Lumen household. Only God knew how the night would punctuate what was certain to be a devastating end to an American family's belief in the proverbial, if not already preconceived, American Dream. For the seven souls in this atypically large, nuclear American family during the Cold War era of the 1980s, this morning would be the last of its innocence. The dawn of reality loomed on tomorrow's horizon.

The house was calm and had its usual foreboding chill. We kept the furnace humming from early October through late April in the two-story, wooden-frame structure. The fourth Sunday of March was another cold, wintry day in the Iron City of Pittsburgh. Our house sat on a hillside in a neighborhood called Etna. Facing the street and on the second floor was a bedroom I shared with my two brothers, and on the first was our living room with double-wide, French-style doors leading to a front porch. In the rear of the second floor were our parents' bedroom and the one and only bathroom. An eat-in kitchen and small back porch were just below where a few steps led to the backyard.

Asleep in the middle bedroom, which looked north to a neighbor's house, were my sisters Gina and Barbara, both older than me. I was fourth in the pecking order, and I considered it a gift to have a younger brother, George, and an older one, Jake. They were snoring in the two other beds, situated somehow—and miraculously, as I see now—in our shared, 13-by-10-foot bedroom. Beneath my sisters' bedroom was the dining room, where we'd gather for holidays and other special occasions, in addition to pulling up a seat just to do homework when space was limited elsewhere.

"Rise and shine! The early bird catches the worm."
Mother continued, "Time to get up! Mass is at 9 AM sharp," she proclaimed, startling my brothers and me, pulling open the drapes and lifting the blinds covering each of the three bedroom windows. During the holidays, we got to decorate one window apiece with our favorite

Pretty Traumatic Love—Michael, Autumn 2008

design. Since Easter was around the corner, we could choose a bunny or an egg. I always opted for a pastel-colored egg. The light shone bright in spite of the cold, and Mother warned, "We can't be late for church!"

"Just ten more minutes." I pulled the comforter over my head.

"Son, look at the beautiful sunshine," she urged as she stripped away my covers. Our bedroom faced east, looking at the hilltop in the distance, where St. Mary's Cemetery stood as a reminder of where all days end. "Last time before I return with the ice cubes!" She had used them in the past, as if it weren't already cold enough in the house.

I blurted out, "Sunday's a day of rest!"

She stopped and turned around just as she was about to leave our bedroom. She warned, "Watch that mouth of yours!"

"I'm not going to just sit and wait in the hallway for a turn in the bathroom."

Mother marched over to Jake's bed—you know, that foot-stomping sound your horse of a neighbor makes in the penthouse above you—and, fed up, lifted off his covers. "Now, Jake, you're the oldest! Set an example and get going. Now!" Mother's commandments resonated like the almighty Ten that were being drilled into us down the street at school.

Surely, I was too young at nine to comprehend fully the underlying dynamics, but I had intuited that there was a kind of military academy to which my parents threatened to send me. They had recreated such a setting in the place we called home.

From beneath the pillow, I overheard mother's continued morning drill. She had moved onto George's bed: "My baby boy, you must get ready for church. We can't be late! God doesn't like latecomers. Rise and shine—you're next in line. There are lots of you to get ready."

Tangent, or "Catching My Writing Breath"

An HIV-positive old lover of mine used to be fond of seizing upon my verbal tangents. He postulated throughout our relationship that I was schizophrenic, like the well-known writer James Joyce, but I reassured him it was just the everyday writer in me, a sufferer of post-traumatic stress disorder (PTSD). I remain on fluoxetine and in psychotherapy for management of my childhood abuse, including sexual abuse by a local roman catholic priest. Pardon this tangential thought process of mine—if it feels that way to you—and please understand that, as the fourth, and overlooked, of my parents' brood, I had to find a way of coping. I created tangents on a dime just to make sure I was being heard and seen—no one likes being ignored or made to feel as such.

A Chore to Start Each Day
One bathroom. Two adults. Three adolescents. Two kids. You do the math, and you get the point. Not unlike other bathrooms found in single-family, lower-middle-class housing districts, ours had a tub with shower, sink, toilet, and linen closet. That space was compromised when I regularly found myself sharing the evening bathtub. If it wasn't with the older brother, then it was with the younger one. Never did I share the shower with anyone during morning hours. At least not in a literal sense, but figuratively, I accommodated a lot and felt it emotionally. After all is said and done, it's what we feel that counts. Imagine a home with no privacy, and you start to get a picture of my childhood.

"Jake! Your time's up!"
On this Lenten Sunday morning, my older brother was getting an earful from our sisters, who were carrying on about who was going to be next. I tried in vain to hold my spot in line. Mother, too, was yelling at the top of her lungs from as far away as the laundry tub in the basement, and continued hollering up a storm of commands from the kitchen. My young ears perceived the distances of her shouts—a rather coarse lesson I was learning as a youngster. Would that I had been exposed to truly operatic voice lessons. But that's what musicians consider a finer art, one performed in concert halls with designated seating capacities.

The smell of pancakes and sausage beckoned, and I thought of skipping the bathroom to warm up my tummy instead. Having tried this in the past, I knew I'd be turned away and told, "No breakfast if

Pretty Traumatic Love—Michael, Autumn 2008

not already showered and dressed!" I sat dejected on the carpet lining the upstairs hallway. Downstairs, my pancakes turned soggy under a lid dripping with condensation.

By the time Jake emerged from the coveted bathroom, our sisters had nearly slit each other's throat. Gina won her first battle of the day, and I confess that I was no match for her, either. Barbara had gone back to bed to stay warm. For the next 20 minutes, I found myself parked—just staring at the paneled wall and hamper of dirty clothes. More yelling up from the kitchen, a diabolical refrain, "Your breakfasts are getting cold!" It felt like I was being teased. I was startled out of my random thoughts by dad.

"Good morning, son," his warm voice filtered down the hall as he came out of his master bedroom. "Why are you sitting there like that?"

I thought to myself, *He must be joking, since he surely knows I had to wait my turn, in addition to the fact that there are no chairs in sight.* "Morning, dad," I said before whining, "Gina's hogging the bathroom again."

My parents' bedroom was adjacent to the bathroom, and, so, before he went another step, he reached out his arm and knocked on the door. "Hurry along in there! You're making the family late."

"Michael," he turned and said, "I need a minute to use the toilet. Just a minute," he reassured. "Your sisters take forever—I know. I'll be just a minute."

"But dad, now you're cutting! No fair."

"You should be glad to have a bathroom. I used to go in an outhouse."

"But we're in a house!" I was confused.

He explained, "An outhouse is where we did our business before indoor plumbing. Times were tough growing up in the Depression and World War II."

"Well, dad, I'm glad we have a bathroom. Can I have my own?"

He smiled. "Your mother and I are working on that. Don't you worry, son."

Gina emerged with a towel wrapped around her head like an Egyptian goddess we had just learned about in social studies class, except that Gina was also wearing a pink bathrobe. I was frightened at the sight of her. You would've been, too. She fancied herself to be a supermodel at 14 going on 15 years old. Her latest diet consisted of cans of Tab and sliced grapefruits for breakfast, lunch, and dinner. I thought then, as I do now, that she had an issue. What kind? That's a question for the mental-health pros!

"Son," dad reminded me, "it's your turn to use the bathroom. Take but a rinse, and be dressed and ready at the table by 8:15. No later!" he commanded. "We must leave plenty of time to get a seat together at church."

Moist Pancakes

"I told you your breakfasts were getting cold," mother said punitively as I pulled up a seat at the kitchen table. The foot of the chair leg got stuck under a piece of linoleum coming unglued. "You kids never listen! Now what's the problem?"

"Good morning, mom." I registered a kindness. "My chair's caught. It's not my fault."

"You overslept. You have yourself to blame. Now eat and behave yourself." She gave order after reprimand before correction time and again. Had I known the word then, I would have barked back, "Stop berating me!"

This was the kind of verbal onslaught I had come to endure and accommodate as a child. It would get far worse in the years ahead, but this first short story of mine is about a singular day in the life of our family that changed everything once and for all.

"Jake, please pass the syrup." I wanted to drown out the sogginess. What kid wouldn't?

"Son, ease up on that surp!" Mother had picked up the local Pittsburgh dialect—in bits and pieces only, to her credit.

I remained silent, eating my breakfast without glancing up from the plate. I entered a world of wishful thinking.

Pretty Traumatic Love—Michael, Autumn 2008

Church—9 AM Mass—Lenten Sunday—March 22, 1981

"In the name of the Father, and of the Son, and of the Holy Spirit," the priest started. It felt to me like any other day at All Saints Church. As a student at the adjacent school, I had to attend mass every weekday at 8:15 AM. In total, I was in that church six out of every seven days! At only nine years old, I had grown tired of such routine displays by fellow churchgoers who obsessed over ritual rather than engaged in mindful praying and singing.

"Son, bless yourself," whispered mother into my right ear. I was on her left; my younger brother George on her right. To my left were Jake and Gina. Next to George, on his right, were dad and Barbara, who managed brilliantly to get the aisle seat. She must have had an exit plan to escape should the need arise.

"I already did," I whispered back, mockingly. I was thinking of how I blessed myself on the inside. She couldn't see it—that's for sure—but God knew. *That's what matters most*, I thought, according to what I was learning next door at school.

"Please, son, make the sign of the cross, like the priest does."

I proceeded to gesture over and over as such, before she grabbed my mocking hands and scolded them, squeezing them to a gentle hurt and fingering my nose. "Once is enough," she said sternly. That was the end of it. Or maybe just the start of what the observant priest on the altar already had in mind for me. After all, he would come to abuse me sexually in the years ahead on the couch in his offices at the rectory, situated between the church sacristy and the schoolhouse's classrooms.

Before I knew it, we were seated and listening to Fr. Rick's homily. He was going on about how people need to pay closer attention to God in their lives. It was similar to most homilies. He asked us to consider the image of a blind—"like a Venetian blind."

"Mom, what's a Venetian blind?" I blurted out.

"Son," she pulled me close enough to whisper, "please be quiet. Just listen."

"The blind of God," he continued, "is how the good Lord sees all that we do. You can see God all around you if you let the light shine. Amen."

I wished to God that the eyes of my parents would see that what I needed was gentle understanding and love at the house we called "home" up the street from this church. Ever since receiving my First Holy Communion in the second grade, I'd looked forward to that part of the mass where pews emptied and everyone broke bread together. On this morning, I had to step over my dad. Usually he didn't go up to receive the host, and we were told it was because he wasn't eligible since he didn't regularly make it to church on Sundays. I never did quite wrap my head around such a rule. In my mind, I knew that, on Sundays when dad couldn't be with us, he was at the steel mill working hard to put bread on the table at home.

I had so wanted to see him receive the Eucharist with me. We fled back into our pew, some knelt and prayed, some slouched back with heads in hands, and I stared up at the pastel-painted rotunda. The painted dove above so captured my blue eyes. The closing hymn was sung as the priest and servers processed down from the altar and past the congregation. As soon as they passed by, each pew emptied. Then fellow parishioners made their escape to the church parking lot. You would've thought the horns were honking in exuberant joy. No! Think again, as you probably already know. These horns screamed out, "Move your car! Get going already!" Impatient and inconsiderate neighbors rushed back to their mundane, dreadful routines. Would that they had connected the dots between being parishioners and acting like neighbors. Can we say "Golden Rule" in unison here?!

My Dad's Last Lunch

"She's not going to that concert!" Mother shouted at father, "That's the end of it!"

Gina had pitted one parent against the other in a classic adolescent ploy to get what she wanted: a ticket to join her friends at a concert by her favorite band, Tom Petty and the Heartbreakers.

Pretty Traumatic Love—Michael, Autumn 2008

"Jane, I know we can't afford to let her go," father shouted back at his wife.

I was seated between my two brothers across from Gina and Barbara, seated on either side of father. Mother, who never sat and joined us at the table, was still fussing about the stove and countertops. Oh, how I wish now—hindsight, like my corrected vision, is always 20/20—that Zoloft had been developed by 1981, since it no doubt could have helped to alleviate her obsessive-compulsive tendencies.

My father kept shouting over our heads, "I know, Jane, I know! The gas bill is due, the light bill keeps going up, and the furnace never stops running! Life ain't just about paying bills, damn it!"

"Gina"—father changed from an angry to a somewhat sad, subdued tone in the blink of an eye as he turned to my sister. "We can't afford to let you go to that concert. Money is tight. Maybe some other time when things aren't so bad."

"I hate this! All of my friends are going! All you and mom ever say is 'No!' and I can't stand it anymore," Gina was yelling now, too. I started feeling empty inside and at the same time stared at my plate of unfinished home fries and Sloppy Joe.

"Where do you think you're going?" mother asked pointedly before I had a chance to push out my chair from the table. Talk about eyes in the back of one's head. Monstrous!

"I'm not hungry. I'm going to put money in my Lenten folder," I explained. I felt as if I should be sure my daily 25-cent contribution had found its way to the appropriate slot of an iconic offertory collection holder.

"You'll excuse yourself when you're done eating! Now sit back down, and eat what the good Lord has blessed you with. Some people don't even have food! You kids don't know how lucky you have it!" Mother had again put the fear of her in me.

Only later in life would I come to understand that the deprived kids about whom she was talking were herself and her fellow orphans she lived with for seven long years in Italy. Mother grew up at the now-defunct orphanage "Madonna Di La Catena, in the City of Gaeta, in the Province of Latina," during and after World War II. This is to quote from public records, not to borrow the style of addressing letters in the play by Thornton Wilder, *Our Town*, a play that I hold dear to my heart. Also, and even more recently, I learned that my mother's very own adoptive family not only physically and emotionally abused her but also violated child-labor laws for nine years after her arrival here in America. That's a story for a different day.

Now, let's return to situating the events in the life of a family not unlike millions of others. What's unique is the way so many life forces came together on March 22, 1981, in the Borough of Etna, and now to pay tribute to Wilder, in the City of Pittsburgh, County of Allegheny, Commonwealth of Pennsylvania, United States of America!

Sacrilege—A Sack of Shit

"Go to hell!" Gina screamed as she ran out of the kitchen. "I hate you!"

"Don't talk like that to your father! You kids are rotten!"

"Jane, don't yell at her like that!" Dad was correcting mother.

"Look, Ralph, you don't need to talk to me like I'm one of your children!" Mother and father were yelling back and forth.

I was forced to clean my plate, but then I excused myself and went to tend to my Lenten folder. The peace and calm I had asked God for at church were nowhere to be found. I sat at a loss for words in the dining room. The kitchen was clearing out. Jake headed to the local playground for handball with his friends. Barbara went upstairs to her bedroom. Gina left the house, still screaming at the top of her lungs and threatening not to come home until late. George pulled up a seat next to me at the dining-room table.

"Bubba"—he had come to use the term of endearment that I had learned from a friend. His family was from Afghanistan, and they were always friendly and nice to me. "Bubba, why do mom and dad argue so much?"

Pretty Traumatic Love—Michael, Autumn 2008

"Bub," I shortened it, swallowing how I felt, "I don't know. They shouldn't."

"You seem sad," George noticed.

"Oh, I'll be okay."

George appeared to disappear, and I decided to place a quarter in every last slot of my Lenten folder. I had enough quarters to do so, and it felt good completing something.

I don't recall anything much happening until it was time to hug dad goodbye as he headed out to work the four-to-midnight shift at a steel mill in Aliquippa, Pennsylvania.

A Final Loving Kiss

"Bye," I hugged and kissed my dad. "See you tomorrow."

"Son, you behave for your mother today."

"I love you, dad," I continued and gave him another kiss goodbye. He kissed me. "I love you, too."

I went to stand by the dining-room window, waited, and watched him make his way out to our car, parked on the street. I noticed only my sister Barbara running out to kiss and hug him goodbye. I didn't notice George or mother. Jake and Gina hadn't returned, and later I learned that they'd waved to dad from the playground down the road as he drove by that cold and gloomy Sunday afternoon.

Ramen Noodle Dinner

I had been sitting on the couch watching television with mother. There were blankets piled on just to keep warm. The living room in which we sat was cold as ever. A steady draft kept the furnace going. The walls of the wood-framed house weren't insulated. I sat pretending to follow the boring movie that mother insisted on watching. I desperately wanted to talk. She would not entertain a word from me. The order—it was always one order after another—was to watch and not disturb her movie. I can't recall the name of it.

Barbara came into the living room and asked if I wanted some dinner. The exact middle child, third in the pecking order, she was taking the initiative to pitch in and make dinner that evening. I jumped at the chance to join her in the kitchen.

She stood tending to a pot of boiling water, and I asked, "Did Gina cause mom and dad to yell?"

"Gina always wants something. That's the problem. She didn't want them to get mad like that. It's not her fault." Barbara sounded like she knew what she was talking about, and I felt the lingering knot in my stomach come undone.

I asked, "What are you making us to eat?"

"Ramen noodles!"

We both loved the taste of the beef flavor, and so that is the meal I remember eating that evening before heading upstairs and getting ready for bed.

Lights Out

It was lights out by 9:30 for George and me. Typically, the older brother would awaken us as he hopped into his bed at 10:30. He had earned an extra hour since becoming a teenager. On this night, my sleep wasn't disturbed one bit. The next time I saw Jake was in the morning, with covers pulled over his head, lying in our widowed mother's bed.

My dad never returned home from work that night, having suffered a massive heart attack and being left for dead on the concrete of an infamous steel mill. The mill would be found in a civil trial to have violated workplace standards by not enforcing its mandatory buddy system. In a technological age before portable life-saving devices (e.g., defibrillating machines) were on airplanes and in workspaces all around this great land, a buddy could have saved my dad's life using good, old-fashioned CPR. Instead, no one went to rescue my dad.

3

Meaningful Survival— Michael, January 2009

January 1, 2009

Here's to 2009! Living the present, planning a future, sharing what's past.
Love, Michael

Thank you, Sam!!
More than these words on these 20 pages can say: I thank God for you.

DEDICATION
I have written these short entries of what will become my memoir to honor countless victims and survivors of abuse.

Names of people other than those of my abusers and family members have been changed to maintain and protect privacy.

I thank many loved ones who have encouraged and enabled me to make it to this point.

Before the Age of Nine

Good Humor. "It's the sound of the ice cream truck! We gotta hurry!" I told my nine-year-old brother, Paul. It was the first summer I had an allowance, and I was going to spend it on my favorite ice cream treats.

Paul, always short on answers, said, "Ice cream will wait."

No way, I thought to myself, and ran ahead, dismissing the ignorance of my older brother. At four years his junior, I knew better. I scurried up two steep blocks—every house sits on a hill in Pittsburgh—to the tune of ice cream truck bells.

Surely life couldn't get any better. How I loved the orange-vanilla ice cream cones. One was not enough, so at a nickel a pop, I used up a dime of my weekly 25-cent allowance. For helping to cut the grass by holding the cord of the electric mower, I earned every penny of it.

By the end of that first summer of allowances and Good Humor treats, I had a plan for the future. I was going to run my very own business. When my birthday rolled around the following April, I had only one thing on my wish list: an ice cream truck. I also knew then that my earning power was well beyond 25 cents a week.

I got it—my very own Good Humor truck at the age of six! Mostly bicycle, part Igloo cooler, all I had to do was attach the insulated cart when I was ready to sell. At all other times, I had the bike to ride in the neighborhood. Soon I was using up my allowance to buy five treats from the real ice cream man. Then I resold them to the kids in the hood who had missed out. I even had my own official work cap and t-shirt. Charging a dime a pop, I made an extra 25 cents. Life was nothing but sweet during my Good Humor days. With my savings from that second summer job, I bought a new bike the next year.

Broken Arm

"Hold on tight, or you'll fall," warned my sister Anna, who was five years older.

Meaningful Survival—Michael, January 2009

I was a nervous wreck and didn't want to be on this seesaw with her in the first place. She convinced dad to let us venture off to the park across from the field where Paul was playing a Little League baseball game.

"I don't want to do this," I pleaded with her. "I'm going to sit on the bleachers with dad."

"You're such a wimp! You total sissy!" Anna taunted.

I went to get down from the seesaw and suddenly found myself flying through the air! Anna, who was rather overweight—the neighborhood kids called her "Fatty" and the like—had bounced down very hard—clearly to knock me to the ground. My right arm snapped across a broken brick sticking out of the concrete playground. I screamed out in pain.

"Pick yourself up," she said without a clue.

"I'm bleeding! This hurts! Get dad! Help me! Someone, please help!"

Anna ran over and was horrified at what was hanging out of my arm. My bones had broken through the skin, and I was trying to deny what was happening before my very eyes.

"We have to get you a bandage, and wait until the game is done," she spoke urgently and with desperation.

"I need dad—please get dad," I begged of her.

"This is the first game ever that dad is seeing, and so we can't tell him now." She had lost her mind for sure. At the tender age of 7, my young mind knew better than hers.

I began to crawl across the ground and roadway to where I knew I could find my dad in the bleachers. It was at this point that a car almost hit me. The car came screeching to a halt, its front bumper inches from my head as I was sobbing in tears. I heard the screams of passersby.

"My child! For heaven's sake, where are your parents?" implored the driver who had rushed to check on me.

I couldn't speak. My sister came running over to explain.

"He must've gotten away. I told him to stay put until after the game."

I was paralyzed by pain, fear, and what I now understand to be the trauma of it all.

"We must get him to a hospital! Where are your parents?" the driver asked my sister.

By then, the scene had grown large enough to distract the baseball game, and soon my dad arrived. From that point on, the world became one blur after another.

In bits and pieces, I had to listen to my dad and sister yell back and forth on the way to drop her off at the house first. I can still picture Anna running out of the car to the side porch and my dad pausing long enough to explain the situation to my mom. *What on earth?* I thought to myself, sobbing and on the verge of passing out from the pain of it all.

On the way to the hospital, with my dad driving the family's blue Ford Torino recklessly in and out of lanes of traffic—he explained that this would be faster than an ambulance, and so, therefore, best—I told how Anna had left me for dead. I was crying uncontrollably. Too busy yelling about having to miss his other son's baseball game, he didn't bother to comfort me.

I heard sirens. I wanted to believe someone cared enough to send the police out to rescue me. Of course, my dad was being pulled over for speeding.

"Mr. Officer, the white handkerchief I tied on the side mirror tells you we have an emergency here," my dad said.

"Sir, I can see your little boy is badly hurt. That's no reason to speed through traffic. Please follow my car to the hospital from this point forward."

It occurred to me the remainder of that afternoon how the good doctor and kind policeman knew better than my family, and what goodness and kindness were in store for me as long as I survived what was fast becoming a hellish childhood.

Runaway

At eight, I had grown to hate the vibe in the house my parents made a home for themselves and my four siblings. There were three bedrooms for seven people: my parents had their own and my sisters theirs. I shared

Meaningful Survival—Michael, January 2009

mine with two brothers. All I can remember are the arguments and yelling matches between the so-called adults, my mom and dad. What's the meaning of those parental palindromes anyhow?

The paradoxes and problems of running such a household are questions for the ages. I just knew that, over at grandma's house were peace and quiet—and an extra bedroom I could call my own on long weekends. One Sunday evening, after returning from grandma's to Greeley Avenue, the name of the street on which my parents' house sat, a light went on in my mind! I was going to pack a bag and run off to live at grandma's house.

I found a small suitcase in the one and only coat closet downstairs, next to the dining room. Pulling a jacket of mine from a hanger so as to hide the suitcase, I began my escape! Tiptoeing up the stairs to my bedroom, I was determined to pack just enough so I could walk with ease the three or so miles to my new home. I opened and closed the dresser drawers ever so quietly. Where was everyone?

I knew that a couple siblings were watching TV with dad before he left for the mill, mom was doing laundry in the basement, and a couple other siblings were outside playing or visiting neighbors. This moment was a gift from God, I felt, and I had every reason to believe I was going to make it.

"Where are you going, son?" my mom called out as I made my way down the side-porch stairs, the gate of freedom, as I saw it, only feet away.

I was busted, and I felt instant anger at her for ruining my plans.

"I'm moving to grandma's house. She said that I'm welcome there anytime."

"The hell you are!" she yelled out, grabbing my arm so hard that I dropped the suitcase.

"I hate it here. All you and dad do is yell at each other."

"Son, you're going to wear that belt again if you don't stop that mouth of yours," she threatened as she tugged at me to follow her up the stairs back into the house.

My dad had appeared at the top of the side porch, belt in hand. I knew what awaited me, and there was no escape from it. *At least not yet,* I thought to myself.

Basement Baseball

As a kid, I enjoyed when my brothers would join in turning our basement into a baseball field. We'd play, almost always to the motherly refrain "Watch out for the hot water tank." The hot water tank was a few feet behind home plate. The pitcher's mound was ten feet away, in line with a drainage pipe that ran some 40 feet-plus from in front of the cold cellar to the laundry room. Second base was beside the workbench and near to a water meter. Fenway Park has its Green Monster; we had our Blue Monster.

The Blue Monster was the aluminum door to the cold cellar. When we were very young, the cold cellar was strictly off limits. I thought, *Is it too cold to survive in there?* Of course, it was where the local farmers used to deposit milk and eggs through a subterranean portal. For us, it was where we kept Kool-Aid to drink between innings.

To the side of the third-base line was mom's hairstyling setup, which she left in place after our dad had passed away. Instead of cuts at the barbershop, we got haircuts from our dad. He had owned a hair salon in his younger years. Lots of memories were in that basement, and we played away a lot of cold days down there. To the right of the first-base line was a big furnace, behind which was a toilet. It made for a luxury dugout!

The electric box designated right field. If you managed to knock an old fuse out, then it was a grand slam. We turned a dark, dank basement into a real field of fun. Our tomorrows could only get better, so we played away our yesterdays. Today is a good day for basement baseball.

Half-Orphaned—Lost and Recycled Family Histories

"Don't be like your father," my father, a steelworker, would often say to me when he sat to help me with my grammar-school assignments. Back then I was not equipped emotionally or intellectually to perceive the self-loathing and embittered identity crisis that my father shouldered.

Meaningful Survival—Michael, January 2009

I felt my dad's anguish. I often said, "I love you, dad," with a childlike understanding of what those three words could do.

The biological toll that my father's financially impoverished family background took was extreme. My father died suddenly of a heart attack on an infamous graveyard shift in a Pittsburgh steel mill, when I was only nine years old. That was the same age my mom was when she arrived on the shores of the United States after a two-month journey from Italy to meet her adoptive family.

During his brief time on this earth—he lived to see only 43—my dad taught me one of this life's most important lessons: to believe in myself and become something. At first, when I was only a kid, I didn't quite know what my father meant. I knew he wanted me to be a good student. Since he had not had the opportunity to finish high school, he wanted most of all to provide me with an education. He reinforced that by helping me with grammar-school homework.

In spite of the bad lessons of abuse, my father did help me to see what he understood. He took me with him to the mill once when he picked up a paycheck. It was the 1970s, well before direct deposit, and my family needed the money. My mom was working full time as well, just to make ends meet. I choose to believe that my dad spent a day off in an effort to teach me a valuable lesson. After all, he could have just dropped me by my grandma's house the way he had on so many other occasions. I recall the drive out to the mill in Aliquippa, Pennsylvania.

On that bright, sunny day, I sat in the front seat of our Ford Torino. It was just the two of us as we drove along the valleys of the Ohio River. After we arrived at the mill, I recall going to the break area, where lots of men were talking loudly. The vivid images of steelworkers are lodged in my mind to this very day. I waited on a bench with some very friendly guys while my dad went to get his paycheck. As we pulled out of the mill parking lot, my dad turned to me and said, "Son, this is your last time in a mill."

Fast-forwarding to junior high school, past the angry stage of my middle-school years that started with my dad's death, I blossomed into a good student and became a compelling leader. In order to be more than just another laborer in my family's social history, I had to rise above the crowd. How was I going to accomplish that?

The whole of my junior-high days, I kept on challenging myself to learn more, even staying after school to learn algebra and get a head start on high school subjects in the eighth grade. Those days of staying after school didn't come voluntarily at first. My string of detentions from my middle-school days was turned around because of the efforts of one of my teachers, Ms. Jones. She saw something in me that I was not able to see myself. That is what makes her a teacher's teacher, and one of the few teachers in my life that I recall. She encouraged me to put my nose in the math book instead of placing my head in my arms and sleeping away another hour of detention. Her and my own efforts paid off when I was awarded the American Legion Award at junior high school graduation as the student who most embodied scholarship and leadership. I had started to become something else.

My only disappointment was that my father was not able to be there to celebrate with me. At such moments, I found myself emboldened and ever more determined to push on and persist in my endeavors. Throughout my early high school days—the same high school where my three older siblings had gone before me—I came to encounter feedback from teachers in dismay of my academic abilities. "You can't be so-and-so's brother," they would say. They had not seen such studiousness and academic determination from a member of my family. I thought in the back of my mind, *If only they knew what solace I take in my studies*, and I wished I could reveal the abuse I had been shamed and threatened into burying. From the time I was 10 years old until the fall of my freshman year in high school, I was sexually abused.

Day of Pain—The Day My Life Almost Ended
On the night of June 20, 2008, I tried to end my life. The doctors have called it a passive suicide attempt triggered by a flashback. Earlier that week I had an argument with my boyfriend, Dirk, after he told me of

plans to leave us and become a priest. His revelation followed shortly after what I had previously told very few lovers. I was abused sexually from the ages of 10 to 14 and subjected to sex at the hands of a powerful and overbearing nearly forty-year-old priest. Now a love interest was telling me that he would rather live his life in secret and that he hated being gay. *Only God will render final judgment on us*, I believed. As the week wore on, I grew sick to my stomach, and my heart ached.

My healthy self wanted to take a mental-health day on Friday, June 20. The workaholic in me put a client's needs first. After a tough day, drinks flowed over at Park Bar as Hank and Jim ordered round after round of shots. Our team had wrapped up just another day at a New York ad agency. I was wasted by the time I got home. When I walked in, there was Dirk on the couch, looking pensive and without offering up his usual kiss. I miss his loving kisses.

Dirk said that he'd be moving out. I was struck by his sudden change of heart. Just a week prior, we'd walked along Bleecker Street and watched the sun set from the freshly cut lawns of Hudson River Park. We talked about a future together. Now Dirk was running from love. He and I said regrettable things on what would become a very dark night. The last thing he said was, "Your life is going to hell," and the last thing I remember saying—and my psychiatrists have assured me that he did not hear it—was "Then it isn't worth living." Later on, I went into the bathroom and swallowed a cocktail of more than 35 pills. Barring a miracle, I should have died.

When I woke up at Saint Vincent's Hospital in Greenwich Village, my older brother was holding my left hand and my younger brother my right. They told me they loved me, and I cried as never before. They had flown hundreds of miles while I was on life support and Last Rites were administered. Dirk had been mindful of the shared catholic faith in which we were raised and summoned a priest after the doctors told him that I might not make it another day. Prayers were answered. When the brain scans and liver tests showed no permanent damage, relief gave way to questions. The primary one is addressed in my ongoing trauma therapy, "What happened the night I tried to kill myself?"

Part of the answer is that I was uninhibited by alcohol and a very potent antidepressant. An even larger part is my Post Traumatic Stress Disorder. The argument with Dirk triggered a flashback to what I endured as a 12-year-old boy. My abuser, Father Rick, now an ex-priest, having been convicted in criminal court for serial child molesting, had violated my family's trust in him in the aftermath of my dad's death. He led my mom to believe that it was okay for him to take me on day trips. One time Father Rick led me to a trail—it was a trail for the blind—telling me he wanted to teach me Braille. On a summer day back in 1983, Father Rick guided my hand across a Braille sign, and then his hand squeezed tight around mine. I felt my breathing change. He forcibly clasped my hand around his penis. I was but a puppet to him. I continued crying out, "No, Father!" His hand squeezed even tighter as he stroked. I was sobbing. My hand felt disgusting. He said that this is what made our love special. No one was ever to know, he threatened, as he often did after abusing me in the church sacristy, rectory, confessional box, and even his car.

Mirror! What's Inside? Confronting Abuse

Every so often, Grace behooves us to reflect. For six months I have been turning bad memories of childhood and adolescence inside out for answers to some of life's questions. In doing so, I have identified good moments as well. You know the kind—like when a light goes on in your mind's eye. That kind of light stays on for the rest of our lives. One such light and its glow beckoned during my recovery this autumn. In the tenth grade at Pittsburgh's North Catholic High School, a teacher, one Mr. David, awakened some classmates and me.

The beauty of having survived my suicide attempt is that I can attest to the healing power within us all through faith in God. It is this insight as I recover that has led me to recollect the light that Mr. David at North Catholic helped to turn on in my mind. Here is how I remember that enlightening day in his U.S. History class.

Meaningful Survival—Michael, January 2009

Mr. David began, "Please open your books to the chapter on the Constitution of the United States of America. What is an amendment?" he asked rhetorically.

I drifted in and out until the point at which our beloved history teacher switched gears and spoke about personal character vis-à-vis social constitution.

He asked, "How many of you have found yourselves searching for answers to life's big questions?" Mr. David challenged us to look into a mirror at home that night while considering some questions: "What defines me? Where will I be after graduation?" He spoke with assurance and confidence that emboldened and encouraged me.

The answers started coming to me the next morning while shaving. I wanted to be anywhere but living in this house after high school. My three older siblings—19, 20, and 21—still called home the same place I did. They had not moved out and on with their lives. I pledged to live up to Mr. David's challenge by committing to do well in school—after all, I was an excellent student, thanks to the head God put on my shoulders—and escape the hells—both physical abuse at the hands of a parent and sexual abuse by a local parish priest—that I endured over the years. On the way to my room and past where my mom had thrown me like a rag doll into a wall the past semester, my answer crystallized: I was going to college. I did it!

I thank Mr. David and only a handful of other teachers like him over the years—including the late Dr. Morales from my days at Penn, for illuminating what it means to believe in one's God-given talents. Instead of being knocked down, abused, and taken advantage of, I have been helped by people in authority, teachers, who let me know how bright my future looked in God's eyes. To recognize the good of this history lesson, especially as I do battle against the very bad memories of abuse during my childhood and adolescence, I thank God for each new day! Depression and PTSD are the residues left by abuse I suffered and endured, and it is the lesson like that from Mr. David's history class that proves timeless.

Thanksgiving 2008

It was a beautiful morning the day before Thanksgiving this year. I had been laughing out loud between sips of hazelnut coffee as I read *A Confederacy of Dunces*, which came highly recommended, and I suggest you read if you need a good laugh. I looked up while turning a page, and there was my ex, Dirk.

He was wearing his hooded, varsity, Abercrombie sweatshirt, emblazoned with a number 28 over the right breast and A&F stitched on the left. His jeans were tight as ever, and his cheeks as rosy and set for the runway as those of any other green-eyed, red-haired model. The fashion houses have no clue what they are missing out on by not signing him.

"I'm so sorry, Tank," he apologized, using this endearing nickname he thought up to get us to laugh along the way of recovering from events in June.

"Thanks, love, but totally unnecessary," I replied and explained that I heard trains were delayed by a terror threat against our beloved Big Apple. Since I had nurtured my capacity for patience in the aftermath of my suicide attempt that summer, I truly didn't mind waiting for Dirk.

He removed his scarf and took off his sweatshirt, and I found myself instantly aroused. Dirk playfully tugged at the navy scarf wrapped tight around my neck. I wore it for warmth and to hide some scars, which seem to bother me randomly and only in public.

"Tank, the usual," he called out to me as I neared the counter.

Rita, the weekday cashier who had remembered our lovers' antics from last winter, asked, "What are you having?"

I told her, "A chocolate-glazed doughnut and sausage, egg, and cheese croissant."

Leaning against the counter, in my baggy sweatpants and baseball cap, I took in the routine of neighbors rushing about for their favorite brew. I got lost in thought.

"Ready!" Rita shouted. "And Happy Thanksgiving to you both."

Meaningful Survival—Michael, January 2009

As I set the tray down, Dirk looked up and very deeply into my eyes. "Tank, it's hard to believe we're here at our favorite café. Having our own little Thanksgiving celebration. This means the world to me."

"Ditto that!" I got him to smile and show me that irresistible space between his teeth, by quoting one of our favorite expressions from the movie *Ghost*. I, unlike the character Sam, played by Patrick Swayze, didn't die. On a serious note, I said to Dirk, "Thank God I'm alive to tell more of my life's story."

I wished Dirk a good time visiting his relatives, and he told me he would keep me in his thoughts and prayers as I journeyed to Pittsburgh the day after Thanksgiving to confront perpetrators of sexual and physical abuse. Flashbacks of heinous childhood abuse had led me to attempt suicide back in June. No more am I a victim to the shame of other people's transgressions. Crimes were committed against me, and the ones to feel guilt and repent for their ways are the perpetrators themselves.

Dirk gave me a look in parting at the café. It was the look that says, "I love you. You're sexy. Let's do it."

I asked him, "You want to come over and see what I've done with the place?"

We walked hand in hand along Bleecker Street. By the time we got to my place, the flame between us had sparked anew. He came upstairs, and we were together like never before.

I am thankful to be alive, that Dirk still is here for me, and that our love is endless.

Another Lancing

Wednesday, the third day of December 2008, at 11:15 in the morning, I arrived in the lobby of Saint Vincent's medical arts building. Just the day before, I got on the schedule of one Dr. Nu, a dermatologist who came very highly recommended. Of concern to me was the raised, inflamed, apparently infected scar on my neck. This is one of the many scars inflicted after I blacked out in the aftermath of swallowing a cocktail of pills back on the night of the summer solstice that year.

"Good morning. How may we help you?" asked the mid-thirty-something receptionist.

"Michael Unglo here to see Dr. Nu."

"Mr. Unglo, please fill out these forms, and we'll need your insurance card and a photo ID for our records."

I passed my cards across the counter, took the pen and clipboard, and got to writing. This is the very kind of demographic information that someday would be captured and stored digitally to reduce paperwork and cut out layers of redundant bureaucracy. These routines at hundreds of thousands of doctors' offices around this great land are what preclude equitable access to medical care by my fellow citizens. Okay, back to this morning's events.

"Mr. Unglo!" called out the physician's assistant, signaling that it was my turn to see the doctor. I had turned in my paperwork about 15 minutes previously.

"Good morning, and thank you." I followed her down the hallway to the fifth examination room on the left.

"What brings you in this morning?" she asked.

"Over this past weekend, I noticed that one of the scars on my neck became inflamed, and over the past couple of days, it has gotten tender to the touch."

"What's the nature of the scars?" she inquired.

I had dreaded this question all morning long, still in trauma therapy for how these wounds came to be signs of my life experiences to date.

"Bad accident back in June, for which I was hospitalized across the street," I quipped so as not to be pressed any further on the topic.

"The doctor will be in to see you shortly," she assured me.

"Good morning, Mr. Unglo, and what brings you in to see me?" the doctor greeted me ever so warmly and with genuine concern in his eyes.

"This scar here on my neck. The one that looks full of pus." I gestured to the spot.

"What happened back in June?" he asked with a welcoming pitch in his voice.

Meaningful Survival—Michael, January 2009

I took him up on the confidence of his office and said, "These scars are from a suicide attempt. Your colleagues across the street saved my life and took excellent care of me."

"Well, let's take a closer look and see what's going on this morning," he calmed me with his words as he peered through a lens. "Looks as if there's an infection in an oil gland beneath the scar tissue. Nothing too serious, but I'll have to lance and drain it."

He did as he explained, and wow! Was my neck sore for the next couple of days! I was instructed to cleanse it with warm water throughout the afternoon and evening, and wait on the culture results. If it turned out to be an infection, he would have prescribed antibiotics. The culture was negative, and so for the time being, I didn't have to worry about undergoing surgery to realign the scar tissue around the oil gland.

I made a holiday dinner for friends the night following the lancing. It was my present to them, showing my awareness that they are here for me, regardless, in good times and bad. Love and understanding are boundless when our hearts and minds are open.

4

Trauma–Michael, July 2009

July 30, 2009

> *To living our dreams out loud!! And proudly so!*
> —Michael R. Unglo

> *Keep dreaming, wishing, and planning.*
> *There's immeasurable power in it.*
> —Laura Smith

> *Trust that still, small voice that says,*
> *"This might work, and I'll try it."*
> —Diane Mariechild

PROLOGUE

I write from the heart and type this essay with soul, and so dedicate this excerpted piece from my "working biography" to people who have experienced victimhood as well as survival. In short, this essay is for every single one of us.

Without the help of others, I'd be dead (I've attempted suicide twice) and gone, and equally forgotten, as mortality is our shared destiny. Our species has an abundance of heroes as well as criminals. Together we nourish each other even as we stomach death and turn a blind eye or two in the face of war and genocide.

Thanks, above all, to God! And for His blessings graced upon us, and for His gifts especially to me: mom's multitudinous love, dad's inestimable energy, Gina's sarcastic wit, Jake's street smarts, Barbara's common touch, and George's determination and indefatigability! Names of people have been changed to mask identity.

Pray for each other as one!

Chapter Zero: A Prosaic Haiku

He stumbled into the corridor at Bellevue. Rendered unaware by a healthcare professional's administration of a nearly lethal dose of a sedative, Ozo had no idea that it was Sunday afternoon, the twenty-eighth of June 2009. In fact, he had no one to defend him from the legions of medical personnel and healthcare professionals (HCPs) at this infamous psychiatric ward attached to New York University in Gotham. He exhorted the nurses and physician assistants to listen and heed his cries to let him go home and sleep it off in the solitude of his apartment. At least there, he could rest in his own bed. Instead, the HCPs finely tuned their robotic selves, and, like robots, they spun away from him and pointed to a chart showing his involuntary admittance. Abandoned, Ozo had no choice but to wait for his day in court to plead sanity. The best Ozo could do that evening was take a sleeping pill called trazodone and swallow as the medication nurse smiled victoriously before lights went out at 11.

Would that this latest healthcare team had not selected Ozo for sedation! A legal battle had already begun over the way Ozo was handcuffed and removed forcibly only two months prior from his Greenwich Village apartment by the New York Police Department (NYPD). This time, however, he was found hanging out his front window—balancing

Trauma—Michael, July 2009

precariously on his hip flexors and penis pointers (e.g., Michelangelo's sculpted David)—on the first Friday night following the 2009 summer solstice. Instead of reaching for help in April after just turning 38, Ozo concocted this second suicide attempt in an effort to highlight the fact that Ozo's actions spoke louder than any of his big words ever could. This night, just a year and a week-plus in time after his first suicide attempt in June 2008, he was attempting a dreadful assault on his own life all over again.

Whatever demons or stray, gray thoughts had taken hold over him were only heightened by the time he awoke on a locked ward. Ozo was consigned to a virtual asylum. I am Ozo. I invite you to join me in reflecting on what it feels like to regain consciousness behind locked doors. Instead of respecting my stated wish to be discharged and not be held against my will, Bellevue Hospital Corporation not only discarded their own hallway-posted patient's bill of rights but also violated larger, broader Constitutional civil rights by excusing one Dr. Beth for sticking Ozo with a syringe full of a sedative (valium or haloperidol). Clearly a violation of ethical codes, Bellevue trespassed against our human rights and shared dignity that is a human hallmark.

Ozo is me, struggling to stay on my own yellow-brick road. My fundamental right to exist as I choose to be and/or become was stolen from me 20 days following my weeklong retreat for writers at the campus college where I plan to complete a graduate degree. The medical thieves at Bellevue should be held accountable for employing HCPs who neglected Hippocrates' warning to "do no harm" in favor of dispensing pharmaceutical binkies. Our right to life ought to include access to unadulterated healthcare and medicine, as well as guaranteed protections against institutionalized assaults on our human dignity. Every human being shares in humanity! Thank God!!

"Rise and shine!" cried a nurse's assistant. Your breakfasts are here. Vitals first! No vitals, then no breakfast. Then meds!" This single-minded, monotonous trumpeter sent me, and most likely a few of the other patients, into an early-morning flashback. My roommates, Rajeev,

Jacoby, and Devann—psychologically, they felt like brothers—were still half-conscious, struggling to get out of bed, and farting up a storm. The air in that room was toxic in spite of our best efforts to get along and pass each day constructively.

For a second time in just three months, my mind had shifted uncontrollably to a distant past. It went in the blink of an eye to my boyhood home. There is where I grew up and weathered a multitude of abusive episodes: physical, emotional, and verbal. Growing up listening to one proclamation after another, I was startled daily by a mother pulling open the drapes and lifting the blinds covering each of the three windows in the bedroom I shared with my two brothers, Jake and George. Mom was proud of running what she jokingly—but she was serious—described as a "boot camp" for her three sons and two daughters, Gina and Barbara. Of course, we were allowed treats, but they didn't come without paying a price for love.

At the age of 38 and reduced to wearing hospital-issued pajamas and a gown, I was still being reprimanded for oversleeping, through no fault of my own. No wonder I played the role of a clown, a sad one, after being awakened by the nurse's refrain as she invaded the room that I shared overnight with a man from Pakistan, a fellow New Yorker, and an undergraduate student lost in his journey away from North Carolina. You can easily imagine the stench. It stank like the kind that gets into your pores! Men do stink to high heaven. Nurse Bellevue kept up her ritual and was parading out of our room and on to where she would utter condescending tunes to the next group of patients caught unaware in their underwear. What possessed her to taunt and tease us? The worst of it was that this adult experience of emotional abuse was in a hospital's psychiatric ward. I have faith that the twenty-first century's curative cocktails and therapies to treat mental illness and insanity do not run over the autonomy and dignity of mental invalids or crush the hopeful power of our shared humanity. In the end, life's as much about spiritual wellness as it is physical and mental health.

Part Two

More Than Just Bad Church Leadership

5

Michael's Suicide and My Introductory Thoughts

My brother died of suicide. It is often said that he committed suicide. He is the one who took his own life. However, I have always found such summary and judgmental statements to be an incomplete description of his life and his struggle, and such statements, yet again, transfer blame from its rightful owners—primarily his abuser, Richard J. Dorsch (please see bishopaccountability.org), a priest who started abusing my brother when my brother was ten years old (Dorsch was about 36 years old then), and the leadership in the catholic church. Even my surviving brother, Paul, has told me that he does not understand why Michael gave up.

Michael did not give up. The manner of his death on his final, fateful night suggests a far deeper story. Haunted by the scars of child sex abuse, which he was working to overcome, he shattered a bathroom mirror in his dorm-like room at Austen Riggs, a mental-healthcare facility in which he was residing in Stockbridge, Massachusetts, took a piece of broken glass, and shoved it into his inner forearm near his left elbow. He then bled to death and was discovered several hours later. Does anyone really want to die this way?

His manner of death requires all of us still alive on this planet to investigate ourselves as a society to see how we operate and how we should respond.

In the days and months that would follow, there were different interpretations of what happened, and the legal system would fail to provide justice, given that the statute of limitations on the original crime—statutory rape and child molestation by a then-priest to our beloved brother—had already passed. As you read this book, you get to decide how your own life will be changed for the better by knowing my brother's story and how you will live and act to make the world a better place.

While my brother ultimately succumbed to suicide and the depression and complex post-traumatic stress disorder (C-PTSD) brought on by child sex abuse at the hands of a priest, I am thankful that he survived his first suicide attempt. Prior to the first attempt, I was not aware of the daily burden and struggles he had. It was extremely difficult to see the man I looked to as a father figure have to go in and out of mental-healthcare facilities the past two years of his life. He was not the brother who I had come to know, but he was finally showing me his true self and the pain and suffering he was battling. I am thankful that I got to know him more the last couple years of his life. He did so much for me throughout his life, teaching me life lessons and inspiring ambitious pursuits, and I am fortunate to have the opportunity to share his life's story with you.

Despite the scars of child sex abuse, Michael did go on to accomplish so much in his life. He did make something of himself. He graduated with honors from the University of Pennsylvania. He was the first in our family to go to college. Professionally, he was a Vice President of Creative Copywriting for a New York medical advertising firm. And, perhaps, most importantly, Michael was a loving son, brother, uncle, and friend to so many. That's probably what we, those who knew him,

Michael's Suicide and My Introductory Thoughts

miss so much now—his loving presence that was always there to inspire success and to make you achieve more than you ever thought possible. Those achievements, which still live strongly in our hearts, are his finest work, and his legacy lives on.

Michael's abuser would always say, "Or else," to him after episodes of abuse to scare and shame him into remaining silent. This book is all about breaking the silence on so many levels so that abuse can be exposed, and we can all learn from the aftermath, and therein, have justice be served, and hopefully, learn and change our ways so that other innocent lives do not have to be shattered by such a horrific crime. We need to be aware in order to change for the better.

Here's your *Or else,* Dorsch, you cowardly piece of shit.

6

Timeline

*S*equencing and timing are an important part of this story. Of course, the perpetrator knew his exact timing, as he was cold and calculating. However, Michael and his family knew only isolated components of the total picture. Before we jump into the story, knowing key background information and chronology will help, and this can be referred to as you read the book.

1937: Paul Unglo (Sr.), Michael's dad, is born in Pittsburgh, Pennsylvania.

1941: Renata Ibride, Michael's mom, is born in Fondi, Italy. She lived in a strict and abusive catholic orphanage in Gaeta, Italy, until the age of seven. The fear of God was instilled in her at a young age.

April 20, 1951: Renee Catanzano (formerly Renata Ibride) arrives in the United States. She was adopted by an Italian-American family living in Swissvale, Pennsylvania (a town in the Pittsburgh metropolitan area).

June 26, 1965: Paul and Renee are married in Pittsburgh.

1966, 1967, and 1968: Michael's three older siblings, Anna, Paul (II), and Frances, are born, respectively.

April 11, 1971: Easter Sunday. Michael Unglo is born.

1975: Michael's younger sibling, Sam Unglo, is born.

March 22, 1981: Michael's dad dies of a massive heart attack at the age of 43.

April 1981: Sexual abuse of Michael begins at the hands of Richard Dorsch, then priest at All Saints Parish in Etna, Pennsylvania (borough just outside of Pittsburgh). Sexual abuse lasted until 1985. Michael was 10 to 14 years of age during the years of abuse.

August 1989: Michael is first in the immediate family to attend college. He attends the University of Pennsylvania and graduates with honors in May 1993.

April 25, 1995: Richard Dorsch is convicted of indecent assault on a 13-year-old boy who said that Dorsch kissed his neck and fondled him during an excursion to North Park (in Pittsburgh suburbs) in summer 1994. North Park is also where Dorsch first abused Michael on The Braille Trail.

Jury Declares Priest Guilty of Molesting Boy on Outing

BY **JAN ACKERMAN.** *Pittsburgh Post-Gazette.* April 25, 1995.

A Roman Catholic priest was convicted of indecent assault on a 13-year-old boy who said the priest kissed his neck and fondled him during an excursion to North Park last summer.

The Rev. Richard Dorsch, 50, did not take the witness stand during his brief trial, which began yesterday morning and ended with a jury verdict shortly before 4 PM.

Timeline

His attorney, Patrick J. Thomassey, argued to the jury that the allegations by the 13-year-old did not rise to the level of criminality required for a conviction of indecent assault.

"They (police) take some affection and some touching and turn it into child molestation . . . and pedophilia," said Thomassey, who urged the jury to view Dorsch's actions as "general human affection."

Assistant District Attorney Christopher Connors urged the jury to reject that argument.

"You are not here to judge this person as a priest. You are here to judge him as a 49-year-old man," he said. Dorsch was 49 when the incident occurred.

The jury of eight women and four men deliberated about an hour and 20 minutes before convicting Dorsch of two counts of indecent assault and one count of corruption of minors. He was acquitted of a third count of indecent assault.

Common Pleas Judge Lawrence J. O'Toole allowed Dorsch to remain free on his own recognizance and set sentencing for June 22.

Dorsch was co-pastor of Risen Lord parish on California Avenue in Brighton Heights when the incident occurred July 26. He has been on administrative leave since his arrest.

After Dorsch was arrested, the Rev. Ronald Lengwin, spokesman for the Catholic Diocese of Pittsburgh, said Dorsch would not be allowed to wear clerical dress, celebrate Mass publicly, or function in any way as a priest until the matter was resolved.

After the verdict yesterday, Lengwin said: "This situation is very painful for the church. Our concern is not only for justice but also, and most importantly, to bring healing to everyone involved, especially individuals and families who have been hurt. We need to do all in our power to reinforce the sacred bond of trust which exists between all of our priests and the people they so faithfully serve."

The victim said Dorsch was a friend of his parents and used to come to his house to watch basketball on television with his father. The boy said Dorsch invited him to the park to play basketball, swim, and golf.

The boy initially told his father and later his pediatrician, Dr. Michael Daly, who, as required by law, reported the allegations to Allegheny County Children and Youth Services on August 23, 1994.

Before testimony began, Connors tried to persuade O'Toole to allow him to present evidence related to a second victim, who claims Dorsch engaged in the same type of conduct with him during a three-year period about 12 years ago. The second victim reported the assaults to police after reading about Dorsch's arrest in the newspapers.

O'Toole said Connors could use the information about the second victim only if Dorsch took the stand and asserted that the allegations were part of an isolated incident.

Priest Gets Jail Term for Assault on Boy

BY **JAN ACKERMAN.**   *Pittsburgh Post-Gazette.*   June 23, 1995.

The Rev. Richard Dorsch said he was sorry for any pain he caused a 13-year-old boy who said the priest kissed his neck and fondled him during an excursion at North Park last summer.

"I thought we were having a good time together. Obviously, I was upsetting him, and I will always be regretful for that," Dorsch said at his sentencing yesterday for indecent assault and corruption of minors.

"My expressions of affection, I know now, were inappropriate."

Weighing the good and the bad in Dorsch's life, Common Pleas Judge Lawrence J. O'Toole came to the conclusion that the priest should have a taste of jail, but not a lengthy one.

O'Toole ordered Dorsch to report to the Allegheny County Jail Thursday to begin serving an 11½- to 23-month sentence.

But O'Toole said he would parole Dorsch July 12 so he could enter a program at St. Luke Institute in Suitland, Maryland, a treatment facility where clergy and others seek treatment for depression, alcoholism, and sexual dysfunctions.

[Dorsch spent 19 days in jail when the minimum sentence was supposed to be 11½ months. Just in case you didn't catch that.]

Timeline

"If you are eligible for the program, I will allow you to go. I do not know who is going to pay for it," O'Toole said.

Defense attorney Patrick Thomassey said the program at St. Luke was six or seven months long and that the Diocese of Pittsburgh would pay for it.

The Rev. Ronald Lengwin, a diocesan spokesman, said Dorsch might be admitted to St. Luke before July 12, but he did not have an exact date.

Dorsch was co-pastor of Risen Lord parish on California Avenue, North Side, when he was arrested in August. The diocese immediately placed him on administrative leave.

In April, a jury convicted Dorsch, 50, of two counts of indecent assault and one count of corruption of minors. Jurors acquitted him on a third count of indecent assault.

At the trial, the victim said Dorsch, who was a friend of his parents, invited him to go to the park July 26 to play basketball, swim, and play golf. During that outing, the boy said, the priest had indecent contact with him.

Yesterday, the victim's mother urged O'Toole to treat the priest "not like a man of the cloth, but as a man convicted of indecent assault."

She said her son was affected by the assault. "He doesn't eat or sleep. He cries a lot and spends a lot of time in his room. His classmates tease him."

She said her son was in counseling and that the family had $2,000 in medical bills that had not been paid by medical insurance.

"A piece of me died the day my son came to me. It doesn't go away, ever," the boy's father said.

Thomassey presented letters from friends of the priest who said he was devout and kind.

Lengwin said the diocese would follow internal policies to determine Dorsch's future.

June 20–21, 2008: Michael's first suicide attempt.

July 2008: Michael first contacts the Diocese of Pittsburgh to report the sexual abuse he suffered at the hands of Dorsch from 1981 to 1985.

Diocese agrees to help support Michael's medical costs (only medical costs) in a sign of good faith.

June 2009: Michael's psychotic break and second suicide attempt.

Summer/Fall 2009: Michael enters full-time residence program ("The Retreat") at Sheppard Pratt, a leading mental-health facility, in Baltimore, Maryland. Diocese of Pittsburgh agrees to cover the cost but complains after a few months that it is too expensive.

Late Fall 2009/Winter 2010: Michael transitions to Austen Riggs, another full-time mental-health program, in Stockbridge, Massachusetts, in response to the Diocese's demand for a cheaper facility. This facility would also become too expensive in their eyes.

March 2010: Diocese of Pittsburgh unilaterally issues a declaration saying that all support payments to Michael need to stop. He has had enough time to heal on their dime.

May 4, 2010: Michael commits suicide.

May 11, 2010: Michael's funeral.

7

The First Time Michael Tried to Tell, My Mom's Complexities, and Family Dynamics

During the summer of 1995, when Richard J. Dorsch was first convicted of child molestation by a jury, I remember that there was much talk about Dorsch in the news and in the family and community. Most of the talk was along the lines of the following: "How could he have done it? Dorsch was always so good to our family. He did so much good."

Despite all the good someone might do, it does not excuse any pain and suffering he causes. It is not a trade. You do not get to do a bunch of good—so the church and society look the other way—in exchange for molesting children. To the contrary, it is clear that Dorsch did good deeds as a way to endear himself and to disguise his real self even further. For that, he should have served his original sentence and more time beyond that for all the other evil done to other boys for which he never stood trial.

The Murder of Innocence

One summer day, I remember sitting in our dining room, where our Apple IIe computer was set up. Only Michael, our mom, and I were home. I was playing games on the computer, and my mom was in the kitchen, adjacent to the dining room. Michael walked into the kitchen. I then heard him ask my mom to sit down, and I started to listen more closely.

He said, "Mom, I know that the boys are telling the truth about Father Dorsch, because he did those same things to me."

There was a long silence.

I do not remember the exact words that followed next, but the spirit of the discussion included the following. My mom was sorry that it happened, as she was one of the ones who could not believe Dorsch could do such a thing. She was mostly in shock. Then, it was decided that, since Dorsch was already in legal trouble, it did not make much sense for Michael to go public. It was essentially decided that Michael would remain in silence, outside of telling immediate family members.

Looking back on it now, that decision was a huge mistake. It took tremendous courage for Michael to tell my mom what happened. As a family, we should have come forward back then. I was only 20 at the time and did not have a full understanding or appreciation of the situation. While I would be the main leader in my family to speak out for Michael in his last couple years and after he died, in 1995, I didn't have the perspective to see the broader, overall problem of the situation. Unfortunately, my mom, who should have been Michael's strongest advocate, always lived in fear of the church—she was a war orphan in Italy until the age of seven and was in an orphanage run by catholic nuns—and her recommended course of action at the time—silence—would turn out to prove deadly in the long run.

While that last statement may sound harsh, I point it out to all the parents out there. You need to be strong for your children and do what they need you to do. You need to be a voice for them. You need to be their advocate. Do not worry about how your family may look. You did not do anything wrong. The catholic church loves to play on guilt

The First Time Michael Tried to Tell, My Mom's Complexities . . .

and fear. Fly above that with truth as your goal, and you can never act wrongly in your response.

To provide further perspective on my mom's state of mind, an excerpt from "A Life History of Renee Unglo," an autobiographically assisted essay that my mother wrote with Michael's help while Michael was in college, follows:

> *My feelings in the orphanage. What those people meant to me . . . I was a small child in the orphanage. I didn't think about anything or anyone, about how or who or what, because I'd never been shown or taught anything about feelings. At that point in my life, I hadn't been taught or educated, so I couldn't know or learn about feelings. I did not have the capacity to even think about anyone or anything. I was a very, very quiet little girl; I never spoke. I just looked and stared into nothingness. That is all I can say of my experience in the orphanage. I was captive in a very dark and scary place. I was given very little to eat, no love, and no kindness. It was like an army: do as I was told, or else it would be a bad time for me. The daily regimen consisted of working, eating, sleeping, and no playing. The orphanage was deliberately kept dark. There was to be no talking, understanding, or getting to know about people and things. I didn't have any of that in my childhood life. I was a big dummy, and today there are times that I still feel like a big dumb head. The nuns and the man that ran the orphanage did not mean anything to me. I was just afraid of all of them; I knew and felt inside myself to keep quiet, listen, and do as I was told. The nuns and the man meant nothing to me except that I had to do as they said.*

My Mom's Birth Certificate

(American Translation of Birth Certificate)
Italian translation of name: Renate Ibride
American translation of new adopted name: Renee Catanzano
Place of birth: Fondi (Province of Rome), Italy

The Murder of Innocence

Year of birth: 1941
Parents deceased during World War II. This child has always been a certified war orphan for her Italian classification. Raised in the orphanage known as Madonna Di La Catena Orphanage, in the city of Gaeta, in the province of Latina, Italy.

My mother's time in a catholic-run orphanage the first seven years of her life says much and provides context around how she grew up and the effects she would transfer onto her own children, however much she might have tried not to. There are several paradigms that were ingrained into my mother that helped neither her own development nor the environment in which Michael, his other siblings, and I found ourselves.

My mother was raised in the old-school catholic environment that made you feel bad about yourself. Any thoughts—not actions—outside of compliance with the ten commandments made you feel badly as a person. You would have to confess your sins to a priest to get forgiveness. The problem with that thinking is that thoughts happen. As humans, we cannot necessarily control our thoughts. There is no need to feel badly about yourself for having a particular thought. What shows responsibility is the ability and choice not to act on all thoughts and to make good decisions.

Notice in my mom's own words, her use of the "or else" paradigm. In the catholic-run orphanage, she was trained to comply and yield to catholic authority "or else." An environment of fear is what was created, and that same fear is still used today by leaders in the catholic church to keep people silent. People are not supposed to go against the church. They are supposed to recognize the infallibility of the pope, put their trust in him, and to comply with the teachings he pushes down.

My mom's silencing of my brother even after he tried to tell her the first time was a direct result of a culture of guilt and feeling ashamed. As a catholic, you are taught to feel badly about yourself. You are a sinner, after all. A negative view of self and feeling badly about yourself are instilled very early on as a child. That, in combination with

The First Time Michael Tried to Tell, My Mom's Complexities...

being taught that the pope and other church leaders are all powerful, is a recipe for disaster. Another classic example of the unhealthy hold church leaders had on my mother was apparent five minutes before we started the press conference at which we initiated a lawsuit against the diocese of Pittsburgh after Michael's death in 2010. My mom pulled me aside and said, "Are you sure we should be doing this? Are they [the catholic leaders] going to hurt our family because of this?" As spokesman for our family, I did not have time to process this fully at the time, as I had to prepare for the press conference. In retrospect, it shows the fear that my mom had in doing anything against the catholic church. That is because the catholic church is very good about making it against the church, and not against the bad leaders in the catholic church. Too often, all the churchgoers feel that an attack on any leader is an attack on them. Therein is one of the major fallacies in the thinking of churchgoers, and they fall into the trap of not holding their bad leaders accountable.

My mother had lost her son to the horrible scars of child sex abuse that were forever imprinted on her son by a priest. Yet, the point most relevant and top of mind for her before we would take a major step in holding them accountable was whether we should be speaking out against them at all. How many readers of this book can identify with my mother and see that they need to change their view to help other loved ones battling with the scars of abuse or to change the culture of whatever organization they are part of?

In a review of Michael's mental-health records after his death, I encountered further evidence that my mom's own abuse that she suffered in the catholic orphanage, which she never addressed or sought therapy for, set Michael up to be abused by Dorsch.

"My mom doesn't know anything about her biological family—and the little she has said about the orphanage was that it was a terribly abusive catholic orphanage where she was routinely beaten. Then she finally gets adopted, but her adoptive father is a total workaholic, and she goes right to work. Also, one of his friends ended up taking advantage of her sexually when she was fifteen. I think her marriage to my dad was the only thing that ever brought her true happiness. She's a master of forgiveness, but she has always had a hard time differentiating discipline from abuse, and she saw me as unruly, and she was physically abusive toward me. She never went to therapy—she turned to the church, and she relied heavily emotionally on the man who abused me."

If you are a parent, are you aware that you yourself may be contributing to your children's grooming for abuse? Have you gone to therapy to deal with your own issue(s)? Or, do you think psychiatry and psychology are things to be avoided (like my mom)? Do you hold a stigma around them and getting help? Are you warning your children about the potential for abuse and creating an atmosphere of open dialogue with your children?

Family Dynamics

A further view into family dynamics and my mother's own history helping to create a culture ripe for a religious (catholic) perpetrator such as Dorsch to exist is found in the Social Work Psychosocial Assessment performed upon Michael's entry into Austen Riggs on October 15, 2009.

Maternal History. Michael's mother, Renee, was born and lived until the age of seven in an orphanage in Italy until she was adopted by two Italian immigrants living in Pittsburgh, Pennsylvania.

Renee's adoptive parents, Rose and Salvatore Catanzano, had three sons (John, Joe, and Sam), when they received a call from Salvatore's sister, Rosinella, who worked in an orphanage in Gaeta, telling them about young Renee. In 1951, at the age of nine [her birthday is late in the year, which can make subtracting years a little confusing], Renee was brought to the United States and immediately began school and working long hours in her adoptive family's business, the Triangle Bar & Grill, a delicatessen and tavern in Swissvale, Pennsylvania. Just a little more than nine years after Renee arrived in their home, Rose died of

The First Time Michael Tried to Tell, My Mom's Complexities . . .

cancer in October 1960, leaving a then 18-year-old Renee in the family home and working long hours for her father.

Where Renee had found a gentle, loving touch in her adoptive mother, she found only a staunch work ethic and cold aloofness in her adoptive father, Salvatore.

By the time Rose died in 1960, the oldest son, John, was out of the house, living locally, and helping to run the family business. Joe, the middle son, had already left the family home and was married with three children.

Renee was closest to Joe, who is still alive and resides in the Pittsburgh area with his wife, Anne, who is struggling with Alzheimer's disease.

Her brother, John, took over the family business in the late 1960s and managed it until his death in the early 1980s. He left behind a wife and two kids, who all live in the Pittsburgh area.

Her youngest brother, Sam, left the Pittsburgh area in the 1980s and works as a chemical engineer and consultant in Georgia. Sam is married to a woman named Sara, and they have no children.

When Renee was 22, she met the patient's father, Paul Unglo, who ran a local beauty salon with his brother. They married when Renee was 23 and nearly immediately began having children.

Two years before Renee married Paul, her adoptive father remarried to a woman named Yolanda. Renee did not get along with her stepmother but made it a point to bring her children to see their grandfather once a month.

As stated, in 1966, one year after their marriage, Renee gave birth to their first of five children, a daughter named Anna. Paul followed in 1967, Frances in 1968, the patient, Michael, in 1971, and Sam in 1975.

Michael states, "Due to the financial demands of having so many mouths to feed, my dad left the salon and started working for a steel company. He, like my mom, had a strong work ethic, and I remember he worked around the clock. When I was nine, he had an accident at work, and while he was lying on the floor waiting for a long period of time for someone to notice and get to him, he had a heart attack and died."

There was a lawsuit after his death, and my mother turned even further to the church for support. Michael states, "She wore black for a long time—too long. But then she went back to work (as a receptionist for a medical practice), and everyone just seemed to scramble around trying to keep busy."

Michael reports having a complicated relationship with his mother and siblings and states, "I don't think they understand that there were family dynamics that accommodated a predator."

Renee has never re-married and lives alone in Pittsburgh.

Paternal History. Michael's father, Paul, was the second of three children born to Michael and Anna Unglo. Both paternal grandparents were born in the United States to Italian immigrants. Anna was born in 1913, was one of at least ten children, and grew up on a working farm outside of Pittsburgh. Michael was born in 1908 and was one of three children.

According to the patient, "My dad had a rough childhood. There were extreme financial pressures and a lot of tension in the home. He had to leave high school in the ninth grade to work full time to help the family make ends meet. I think he always resented that."

The patient's father, Paul, opened up a beauty salon with his younger brother, David, in the early 1960s, and it was during this time that he met the patient's mother, Renee.

The patient states, "But he and mom started having kids, and he needed to do something that would be a little more stable—so he began working for a steel company. My aunt Frances died in 1967, and the story goes that my grandfather was so brokenhearted that he died just three months later. Uncle David died of AIDS in 1988—seven years after my father died. My grandma didn't die until 1993—so she buried her husband and all three children."

About his father, the patient states, "He was a man's man. I just never really took to him, but I think he ultimately just kind of left me

The First Time Michael Tried to Tell, My Mom's Complexities . . .

alone. I don't remember much, but my brothers and sisters tell me he and mom had a very loving marriage."

My mom, while loving at times, was also very abusive and angry at times. She probably imitated behaviors done to her, and thereby continued the cycle of abuse and helped to create the potential for Michael's own abuse. I recall times when my mom chased and beat Michael with a Wiffle ball bat because she was upset with him. She also chased and beat him with a hanger for tormenting me one time. Another time, she chased him into her room and pushed him through the drywall between two studs in the wall. The hole in the wall would go unrepaired for several years, and unfortunately, be a nightly reminder of the incident, as that is where Michael studied most school nights. Due to space constraints in the house, the "study desk" was set up in my mom's bedroom, where Michael or I could study quietly. It was a reprieve from an otherwise usually noisy house, but at the same time, it was a reminder that we were under her domain. And, in Michael's case, two feet from the desk was the hole in the wall where she had pushed him through.

8

Dorsch's Attempt on Our Oldest Brother, Paul— but No One Takes Heed

A few years after Michael passed away, I asked Paul to reflect on his own experience with Dorsch. Paul agreed and provided me with the following.

> "I was the oldest son. I enjoyed being an altar boy under Sister Mary Paul. She was a wonderful lady and a great teacher. Many months had passed, and then our parish got a new assistant priest named Dorsch. Sister Mary Paul was very upset. She came to me and told me that I would be retested for what I already did very well. You see, I had a paper route in the morning before Mass and school. So, this new priest was telling me that I would be retested after a while serving Mass with him. The days came and went. Then after Mass one morning, Dorsch told me he wanted to see me. It was just me and him in the sacristy. He was sitting on a chair and asked me to

come over. That is when he grabbed me and told me to sit on his lap. I told him I would rather stand. He told me he wanted to review for the altar-boy test. I told him I would still like to stand or sit in my own chair. He then forcefully turned me with my back to him and sat me in the middle of his pelvis. Not to one side or the other of his lap, the middle. He had been aroused by this from what I felt and because he held me there.

For some reason that morning, the pastor of our church, Father Michael Pollack, walked in and said, "What is going on in here?"

I immediately told Father Michael Pollack what was going on. He ordered Dorsch to let me go. Father Michael Pollack told me I did not have to sit on his lap or anyone else's lap for any altar-boy test. Father Michael Pollack saved me from God only knows what that day. I went home and told my dad and mom. I was told by my mom that I was reading into something that was an innocent misunderstanding."

The incident above took place shortly before my dad died in 1981. So, here you have Paul telling his mom and dad. Dad told Paul to stay away from Dorsch. Mom told Paul that it was a misunderstanding of Dorsch's affection. Neither my dad nor mom, nor Paul, told Michael (or me) as a heads-up to stay away from Dorsch.

Why would my mom trust Dorsch blindly after knowing that Paul himself already had almost become a victim of Dorsch? Why did she not prevent any one-on-one situations where Dorsch was isolated with one of her children?

I like to reflect on people's ability to recognize and accept both good and bad in others. Evil can exist in seemingly good people. Just because people have done good does not mean that they have not done or will not do bad. Too often, in our minds, we want it to be one or the other, and we cannot accept that both are true. We need to evaluate each action on its own merits. My mom, for example, could not reconcile the good Dorsch did for the family with how he could possibly do bad. People doing good does not negate or excuse any bad they dream up and do.

Part Three

The Battle with the catholic church

9

Why catholic-Related Words Appear in Lowercase: Beware of Authority

One of Michael's first days of school as a youngster at All Saints School in Etna, Pennsylvania.

The Murder of Innocence

Power tends to corrupt, and absolute power corrupts absolutely.
— John Emerich Edward Dalberg-Acton

Have you ever asked yourself whose interests the pope really protects? Who pays for all the maintenance, gold, and upkeep involved with saint peter's basilica? Did God and Jesus Christ, if they exist, really want so many riches to go to maintaining physical assets instead of helping those in need? My brother's experience with leaders in the catholic church show that they are in it for themselves. They protect their own positions, not the interests of those whom they hurt and harm.

Ronald P. Lengwin, who is on staff at the diocese of Pittsburgh, when interviewed after my brother's death, outright lied. He stated the following in a television interview the day we brought suit against the diocese of Pittsburgh on July 30, 2010, "The Diocese of Pittsburgh cannot accept that any action [by] the Diocese contributed to or was responsible for his death." You can watch him at the following link: https://m.youtube.com/watch?v=gJksUJumZIE. He noticeably stutters trying to read a prepared statement (he looks down to see what he is supposed to say) and cannot even articulate a grammatically correct sentence because he is lying.

The diocese will be quick to point out that they paid more than $300,000 for Michael's mental healthcare after his first suicide attempt in June 2008. However, that was not enough, and they unilaterally told Michael that they had paid enough and would not continue to help him. In the same television interview, when Lengwin was asked about cutting off funding, he said, "It was a matter of review because we, we need to continue to be responsible also in terms of the funds we provide and to, to make sure there is a need there." The same interview explains that Lengwin said that funding was never cut off, and Lengwin acknowledged that the diocese still provides Dorsch, Michael's abuser,

Why catholic-Related Words Appear in Lowercase: Beware of Authority

with a monthly stipend. That is correct—the abuser's funding and living expenses were never interrupted, but the victim had only an arbitrary amount of time to heal as dictated by the diocese. The diocese also takes pride in noting that Dorsch was not defrocked. Dorsch withdrew himself from the priestly ministry in 1996 (a year after he was convicted of child molestation). That says it all. The diocese did not defrock a convicted child molester. They let Dorsch retire so that he could collect a monthly stipend. How convenient!

In the following chapters, while I will provide further insight into the diocese's self-serving views as articulated in their own communications (mostly letters to us), the document that is the clearest in showing how much they lie is the one that refutes their saying that they never intended to cut off funding while my brother was still alive. The correspondence below clearly shows that it was not just "a matter of review." Michael and I were sent a full and final release to sign on March 17, 2010. Funding was to be cut off at the end of April, and Michael was clearly aware of that fact prior to his death on May 4, 2010. William G. Batz was assigned to deal with me after David A. Zubik, bishop of Pittsburgh at that time, refused to deal with me directly.

From: Batz, William G.
Sent: Wednesday, March 17, 2010, 2:23 PM
To: Unglo, Samuel J
Subject: Michael's Discharge

Sam,

We have had thoughtful discussions here about the best way to proceed in dealing with your brother Michael's transition from Austen Riggs, and I appreciate your thoughts on a budget for his upcoming needs.

As I indicated last week, the diocese is unable to provide funds for the purchase of a home. You also questioned if Michael could join the diocesan employee medical program. The program rules do not allow for non-employees.

You raised up again the offer made by the diocese before Michael entered Austen Riggs. We had offered to settle a final sum of $250,000 on Michael for his future needs. That offer was declined. However, as you pointed out, if the Unglo family had accepted that offer, then there would be a residual amount of approximately $74,530 remaining for Michael's future care. This is not materially different from your budget estimate of Michael's transition needs, excluding the house down payment and contingent items.

Thank you for the specifics of Michael's budget which you sent. Of course, how you and your brother ultimately apportion any funds for housing, transport, counseling, etc., is something we leave to you, but it helped us to understand Michael's needs.

The diocese has already expended hundreds of thousands of dollars on Michael's recent care, but we told you that we would honor our commitment to support treatment at Austen Riggs until April 2010. Assuming Michael leaves Austen Riggs on March 25th, you estimated that the balance would be about $29,045.

So, as you point out, if the diocese honors its commitment, it should be willing to provide approximately $29,045 for Michael's future needs. Or the diocese could accede to your request that we reconsider our earlier offer, and provide the balance of the $250,000, or approximately $75,000.

Out of concern for Michael's care, the diocese will agree to issue one final payment of $75,000, provided two things:

First, we would require you and Michael to sign (with witness and notary) the attached statement which acknowledges your willingness to release the diocese from any and all future claims.

Second, we require a statement from Austen Riggs that Michael is capable of signing the statement.

Provided you are willing to provide these two documents, we will issue and send a check for $75,000 to you or your brother at the address you specify. If you accept this offer, please provide the two documents to me as soon as possible, and we will issue the check. If you decline this renewed settlement offer, we will finalize accounts with Austen Riggs upon Michael's departure, and calculate and send the residual amount to Michael at the address you provide for that purpose.

Sam, I thank you for your recent acknowledgment of the fact that the diocese has overextended itself in Michael's case. I know you will accept this offer in the spirit of concern in which it is presented, but also with the realistic knowledge that, as Michael's in-patient treatment ends, the financial support of the diocese will definitively conclude at this time as well. I cannot over-emphasize that the diocese has already expended major sums, and does not have further resources to provide. With all due concern for Michael, we will not entertain further expenditure requests. I need to highlight this fact so that you and Michael can make the best decision for him.

Bill

Enclosure below (the Full and Final Release):

FULL AND FINAL RELEASE

I, Michael Unglo, being of full age and of sound mind, for and in consideration of the sum of Seventy-Five Thousand ($75,000.00) Dollars paid to me in hand by the Roman Catholic Diocese of Pittsburgh, I hereby forever remise, release and discharge the Roman Catholic Diocese of Pittsburgh, Bishop David A. Zubik, Archbishop Donald W. Wuerl, and any other persons or entities affiliated with the Diocese, its successors and assigns, of any kind of liability, claims, causes of action, damages, costs, expenses, or demands of any kind whatsoever in law or in equity, and specifically from any claims or joinders for liability, contribution or indemnity against the Roman Catholic Diocese of Pittsburgh and parishes within the

Roman Catholic Diocese of Pittsburgh that I ever had, now have or which I may have by reason of bodily injury and personal injuries and damages sustained by me, and the consequences thereof, known or unknown, foreseen or unforeseen, arising or which arise as a result of or in any way connected with the incidents of alleged sexual abuse which have formed the basis of my complaint to the Diocese of Pittsburgh, against a former priest of the Roman Catholic Diocese of Pittsburgh.

The aforesaid sum being paid by the Roman Catholic Diocese of Pittsburgh shall constitute payments for damages on account of personal injuries or sickness, within the meaning of Section 104(a)(2) of the Internal Revenue Code of 1986, as amended, and therefore not taxed as income.

It is further understood and agreed that the acceptance of this sum is in full accord and satisfaction of a claim against the Roman Catholic Diocese of Pittsburgh.

It is further understood and agreed that this is a complete release agreement and there is no other written or oral understanding or agreement directly or indirectly connected with this release. Any liability for payment of any liens or claims by any health providers, attorneys, etc. that are as a result of this injury are my personal responsibility.

I declare that I fully understand the terms of this release and receipt of the sum of money above stated, and that I further understand that any claims that I may now have are barred by the applicable state law in effect in the Commonwealth of Pennsylvania. I further understand that at some time in the future, laws may change, and that the Legislature of the Commonwealth of Pennsylvania could at some time in the future pass legislation that could allow a window or period of time within which to file claims that are presently barred by the statute of limitations, however, by signing this release and receiving this sum of money, I understand that any and all claims are barred and forever precluded.

Why catholic-Related Words Appear in Lowercase: Beware of Authority

I acknowledge that receipt of this sum of money is the sole consideration for this release and I voluntarily accept the same for the purpose of making a full and final release of my above-mentioned claims.

IN WITNESS WHEREOF AND INTENDING TO BE LEGALLY BOUND HEREBY, I HAVE HERETO SET MY HAND, this _____ day of _____ 2010.

_____
MICHAEL UNGLO

WITNESS

County of _____)

                            SS:

State of _____)

On this _____ day of _____, 2010 before me personally appeared Michael Unglo, known to me or satisfactorily proven to be the person who executed the above instrument and that he severally acknowledged to me that he executed the same for the purposes therein contained.

Witnessed and acknowledged further by:

_____
Samuel Unglo,
Brother of Michael Unglo, for whose benefit this agreement is made.

Bill's letter, as usual with the diocese and the catholic church, missed the mark. I never said that the diocese overextended itself. All along I tried to reiterate to the diocese via letters and calls that the victim should get whatever he needs to heal—plain and simple. The sickness of the diocese and the catholic church is that they knowingly provide for child sex offenders such as Richard J. Dorsch long after they are convicted while simultaneously cutting short the funding of victims who are trying to recover from the actions of such perpetrators.

Fortunately, neither Michael nor I ever signed the despicable "Full and Final Release" that was offered. My brother had the utmost dignity and would not sign anything that compromised and silenced the real truth from shining through. What is the price of innocence?

Zubik, Batz, and Flaherty would never back off of their push to end all funding, even in the face of the following letter from Michael's main doctor at Austen Riggs. They paid for this expert opinion, which they chose to disregard.

```
Austen Riggs Center
25 Main Street, P.O. Box 962
Stockbridge, MA 01262-0962
Telephone: (413) 298-5511, Fax: (413) 298-4020
www.austenriggs.org
```

> Dr. William G. Batz, General Secretary
> Diocese of Pittsburgh
> 111 Blvd. of the Allies, Pittsburgh, PA 15222
>
> April 5, 2010
>
> Dear Dr. Batz:
>
> We are recommending Michael Unglo's continued treatment at the Austen Riggs Center, which we consider medically necessary at this time. In his treatment with us, Michael has worked hard to decrease his vulnerability to emotional dysregulation and suicidal behavior associated with his diagnosis of Post-Traumatic Stress Disorder (PTSD, Primary Diagnosis); Psychosis Not Otherwise Specified; Major Depressive Disorder, Recurrent, In Partial Remission; Dysthymia; Alcohol Abuse; and Personality Disorder Not Otherwise Specified; related to history of childhood sexual abuse. Though Michael has made significant progress in achieving stabilization again, there is still

a need to grapple with the determinants of his problems over more time, given the severity of Michael's symptoms, his sexual abuse history, and his history of two serious suicide attempts in the past 22 months.

Michael's psychological testing indicates that he has clear vulnerabilities to suicidal behavior when he is overwhelmed by emotions that he is not able to regulate. Currently, Michael's high level of emotional dysregulation, which has increased over the past month, combined with his active trauma symptoms, necessitate the continuation of his current treatment at a residential level of care. Michael's emotional instability has been compounded by the retraumatization he experienced as a passenger in a motor vehicle accident on March 24. In this accident, a pedestrian threw himself in front of a car in which Michael was riding in the front passenger seat, involuntarily including Michael in the pedestrian's apparent suicide and placing Michael at risk of injury or death in this collision. At the time of this accident, Michael was in a psychologically vulnerable position after experiencing a degree of anxiety and emotional instability that led to the postponement of his previously planned discharge. Since the accident, Michael has experienced additional and recurring trauma symptoms, including flashbacks and dissociative symptoms. At this time, Michael is at high risk of further psychological and emotional instability, and his ongoing treatment should not be disrupted. We recommend continued residential treatment so that Michael can stabilize following this acute trauma and progress in psychotherapy to a point at which he can stably discharge to outpatient treatment.

Based on our clinical assessment we recommend six months of additional residential treatment at Austen Riggs, with a reassessment after six months to determine Michael's need for further residential or outpatient treatment. We recommend that Michael transition to one of our residential step-down programs prior to his discharge, as this will allow him to have a more gradual transition to independent functioning, and lower the potential for destabilization following his discharge. Though this recommendation was included in Michael's original referral to Austen Riggs, his need for higher-level care has not yet allowed such step down. When Michael transitions to a step-down program in the future, this would lower the treatment cost per day. However, at this time we cannot predict when Michael will be ready to make this transition. The cost of Michael's continued treatment at his current level of care (Inn Residential Program-Group) is $785 per day, $23,500 per month. In order for Michael to remain in treatment at Austen Riggs, a signed guarantee of payment must be received by April 15, 2010.

Please contact Michael's therapist, Dr. Lee Damsky, at 413.931.5304 with any questions regarding this recommendation. Please contact Nancy Peck (413.931.5310) or Cynthia Racine (413.931.5207) for information regarding payment arrangements.

Sincerely,
Lee Damsky, Ph.D.
Psychotherapist

Jane G. Tillman, Ph.D., ABPP
Team Leader

Why catholic-Related Words Appear in Lowercase: Beware of Authority

Even after providing a medical doctor's professional opinion that Michael was in no way ready for a full and final release, the diocese again reiterated its stance, one week later:

```
From: Batz, William G.
Sent: Monday, April 12, 2010, 4:45 PM
To: Unglo, Samuel J
Cc: Flaherty, Rita E; Joyce, Rita F
Subject: Austen Riggs etc.
```

Dear Sam,

Since I was unable to reach you by phone just now, I thought I would drop this email. I am cooped in an all-day meeting tomorrow.

We have about three weeks yet until April 30th to finalize what happens next at Austen Riggs, but in the end, that is naturally up to you and your family to decide with Michael. Our offer still remains. After Michael completes his treatment through April 30th, we would be willing to give you/Michael $75,000 for you to expend for his future needs. We ask that you return the Release with Michael's signature.

I reiterate this proposal since we cannot know how long Michael will actually wish to remain at Austen Riggs or what level of care . . . full, stepped down, etc., . . . he will receive. At $785 per day, the sum we offer would last 96 days, but at the stepped-down rate, much longer. Our goal is to give you flexibility and not insert the diocese into the specific decisions of what is best for your brother.

I was sorry to hear of Michael's recent traffic mishap with the pedestrian. That's the last thing he needed.

Best wishes,
Bill Batz

So, after medical experts stated what was needed, the diocese still proceeded to pressure, in actions and words, for a full and final release. Again, all this was done by them while they were still providing uninterrupted funding for the perpetrator who caused the mess from the start.

How catholic Schools Can Instill Fear of Authority

I recall times in catholic grade school and high school when priests, nuns, or brothers would squeeze my arm if I had done something wrong. It might seem like a small violation of personal space. However, when you grow up in a culture of accepting everything the church says, you feel hurt by the act, and you are made to feel that you are wrong. The fact is you might have done something wrong (sometimes not), but that does not permit anyone to harm you physically against your will. Are we mindful of those seemingly small things that say so much about how we are acting?

I recall when Michael was still alive and with Lynne (my wife), Luke (my son), and me one Sunday for church. Michael would not always go to church with us, but this Sunday he did. Luke was about three years old. We were already in the cry room, and I was getting upset with Luke because he was crying. In my own repeat of behaviors done to me, I overreacted, grabbed Luke by the arm, walked him out of the cry room and proceeded to tell him that he was not behaving. What a crazy expectation that I had! First, that a three-year-old should sit silently for an hour (because I was forced to do that growing up), and second, that a three-year-old should be quiet in a cry room. Michael had followed us out and saw what had happened. He stood up for Luke and told me that I was acting like an ass and that I should not be hard on him the way I had been. As this was after Michael's first suicide attempt, I took his advice, trying to reflect on what I had done. He got me to change my thinking then, but in retrospect now, I get even more his point and why he was so upset—I was acting the same way that some of our shared abusers had.

Why catholic-Related Words Appear in Lowercase: Beware of Authority

The Day I Walked Away from catholic Propaganda

It was a couple months after Michael had passed away, and I still wanted to believe that the leadership of the catholic church could do the right thing. I found myself sitting in church wondering how an institution that is supposed to stand for righteousness acts so evil. As the priest finished an unusually short homily, the reason for that became clear: To show a video designed to highlight all the good that the catholic church and catholic schools have done. In return, you should donate more money to them. They left out the part about how they continue to pay for the retirement packages of convicted child molesters. And, they even went so far as to include how they have always been at the forefront of science. Wow! At that moment, I couldn't take the hypocrisy of it anymore. I got up, left the church, and have not been in a full mass since. Does anyone remember how the catholic leadership treated Galileo?

February 13, 1633 (source: https://www.history.com/this-day-in-history/galileo-in-rome-for-inquisition)

On this day in 1633, Italian philosopher, astronomer, and mathematician Galileo Galilei arrives in Rome to face charges of heresy for advocating Copernican theory, which holds that the Earth revolves around the Sun. Galileo officially faced the Roman Inquisition in April of that same year and agreed to plead guilty in exchange for a lighter sentence. Put under house arrest indefinitely by Pope Urban VIII, Galileo spent the rest of his days at his villa in Arcetri, near Florence, before dying on January 8, 1642.

Galileo, the son of a musician, was born February 15, 1564, in Pisa, Italy. He entered the University of Pisa planning to study medicine but shifted his focus to philosophy and mathematics. In 1589, he became a professor at Pisa for several years, during which time he demonstrated that the speed of a falling object is not proportional to its weight, as Aristotle had believed. According to some reports, Galileo conducted his research by dropping objects of different weights from the Leaning

Tower of Pisa. From 1592 to 1630, Galileo was a math professor at the University of Padua, where he developed a telescope that enabled him to observe lunar mountains and craters, the four largest satellites of Jupiter, and the phases of Jupiter. He also discovered that the Milky Way was made up of stars. Following the publication of his research in 1610, Galileo gained acclaim and was appointed court mathematician at Florence.

Galileo's research led him to become an advocate of the work of the Polish astronomer Nicolaus Copernicus (1473–1573). However, the Copernican theory of a sun-centered solar system conflicted with the teachings of the powerful roman catholic church, which essentially ruled Italy at the time. Church teachings contended that Earth, not the Sun, was at the center of the universe. In 1633, Galileo was brought before the Roman Inquisition, a judicial system established by the papacy in 1542 to regulate church doctrine. This included the banning of books that conflicted with church teachings. The Roman Inquisition had its roots in the Inquisition of the Middle Ages, the purpose of which was to seek out and prosecute heretics, considered enemies of the state.

Today, Galileo is recognized for making important contributions to the study of motion and astronomy. His work influenced later scientists such as the English mathematician and physicist Sir Isaac Newton, who developed the law of universal gravitation. In 1992, the Vatican formally acknowledged its mistake in condemning Galileo.

It took 359 years for the Vatican to admit it was wrong in how it handled Galileo. Just amazing! What a bunch of morons! Divine, self-righteous stupidity!

10

The Perpetrator: Richard J. Dorsch

> To be nobody but yourself in a world which is doing its best, night and day, to make you everybody else means to fight the hardest battle which any human being can fight; and never stop fighting.
> —E. E. Cummings

*Michael's abuser, Richard Dorsch,
giving Michael his first holy communion.*

When my brother Paul and I met with David A. Zubik and Rita Flaherty in December 2008, I requested that Dorsch write a letter of apology and explanation to Michael, as well as a separate letter to our family. Below is each of those letters, as well as Flaherty's letter confirming that Dorsch wrote these letters.

The Perpetrator: Richard J. Dorsch

Dear Michael,

I have been told that your family has requested that I send a letter about the concerns you have expressed to the diocese. This is the hardest letter that I have ever written; but it is one that, after much reflection, I want to do.

It has been brought to my attention that you have been having a difficult time dealing with memories of our times together when you were younger. This is very painful for me to hear that this has happened to you. You and your family were among the best friends I had, both when you were all growing up and continuing through later years. Michael, I never intended to ever do or say anything that would upset you in any way. Your friendship and excitement about our getting together meant a lot to me. I apologize to you for not allowing those memories to be anything but what you wanted.

I have come to see myself as a very imperfect human being, with many faults, weaknesses, and insecurities, some of which have become apparent to me now as I look back on my life. Although there was a part of me that believed I was having a positive effect on people who were a part of my life, I now also realize there was also a self-serving side that missed the possible negative impact I may have had on others. To the degree that that happened between us, please know that I am very sorry and never wanted anything hurtful to happen to you. I am not trying to justify or explain away anything I said or did that was inappropriate or wrong. I just am trying to say that the difficulties you are going through now are unfair to you, and I am greatly distressed to hear that I am part of what you are going through.

You have been blessed with a very loving family. That is why they approached the diocese in hopes this letter might become a part of your healing. Continue to receive their love and support, as well as that of all your friends, as you try to move on in your life and believe in your inner goodness and value. You always had a sense of wonder and enthusiasm in life. I hope that can be restored and you can somehow allow your experiences in life, both positive and negative, to allow you to continue to grow personally and have an effective impact on all the people who are now a part of your life. You have so much to offer. Please do not allow my failures to keep you from making progress and being a success in life.

Sincerely,
Rich Dorsch

TO: Sam Unglo
FROM: Mrs. Rita E. Flaherty, M.S.W., L.S.W.—Diocesan Assistance Coordinator
DATE: January 21, 2009

Enclosed is the sealed envelope that I received from Richard Dorsch. I send this letter with some trepidation, not knowing its content. I pray that whatever this letter says, it will help to bring some healing to you and your family. Depending on how the letter is written, I would be cautious sharing it with your mother. If after reading the letter, you do not feel that it would be helpful for her to read, I would suggest that you not show it to her. I am sure that she carries a lot of heavy feelings that she allowed Richard into the lives of her children not knowing where his connection to your family would lead.

The Perpetrator: Richard J. Dorsch

You and your entire family are in my prayers. I know that you and your brothers only want to be healed and to put this all behind you. Just be aware that each person carries the pain of abuse with them in a different way. What is helpful to one person may not help another. I know that you do all of this out of love for your family so I know that you will be sensitive to everyone involved.

Keep in touch and let me know if this letter was of help to you.

To: Members of the Unglo Family:

I am sending this letter in response to your request that I write to both Michael and all of you about the concerns Michael has brought to the attention of the diocese. I have already sent a separate letter to Michael.

Your friendship and acceptance of me was always an important part of my life for so many years, especially for the special events in your family life. This is true in both the earlier days and also later, when the children were grown up. I realize that it is not easy for any of you to experience any comforting feelings now about those times because of what you are going through.

When I was with Mike, my hopes and intentions were always that he would enjoy our times together. He always has such a life-affirming attitude toward everything and brought much joy into the life of all who knew him. I never wanted anything to happen that would ever hurt him then or anytime in the future. I deeply regret whatever I said or did back then that is causing him his present distress. But his present discomfort is real, and that is what matters. I do not pretend to be able to explain or reconcile these two realities. I realize that I am a flawed human being who has at times missed the impact of my words or actions on others. I should have been more sensitive to him and acted more responsibly when we were together. But Michael's well-being is what is most important at this time. Because Michael is an important part of each of your lives, his pain is also your pain. I want you to know that I am also sorry for what is happening to each of you and for my part in causing any of that pain.

I told Michael that I hoped he could begin again to believe in his inner goodness and the positive impact he can have in the lives of so many people. I know from personal experience how much your kindness can mean to a person, and I ask you to continue in your support and love for Michael in this difficult time in his life. My own family has helped me get through very stressful times. Your strong family ties can not only be a help for him, but also for each other at this time.

Sincerely,
Rich Dorsch

This is all truly alarming. All Dorsch can muster to admit his guilt and shame is, "I deeply regret whatever I said or did back then that is causing him his present distress." Did he forget that he forced my brother to give him hand jobs and blow jobs? He also clearly forgot about putting his dick in Michael's ass. Dorsch is a piece of shit.

The Perpetrator: Richard J. Dorsch

Michael wrote a formal response to the diocese of Pittsburgh after receiving Dorsch's supposed apology:

TO: Rita Flaherty
CC: Sam Unglo, Paul Unglo II, Anna Dzikowski, Frances Samber
FROM: Michael Unglo
DATE: January 27, 2009, 9:02:00 AM EST
SUBJECT: Dorsch letter to me/us

Good morning! Hi Rita,

This is just to touch base with you.

It is now clear from Dorsch's letter—which I have shared in its entirety with my family—that my request was mishandled by you/Bishop Zubik's staff. Dorsch's first paragraph starts, "I have been told that your family has requested . . ." It's clear that Dorsch was not told that I, Michael Unglo, an individual victim of his sexual abuse, any episode of which he fails to mention at all explicitly in his letter, requested the letter. How was my request relayed to Dorsch? By you? A church lawyer? The bishop himself? Why would good people such as yourselves knowingly choose to try and protect a convicted criminal—may God have mercy on your souls! I pray for you, too.

I feel the need to refresh your memory. At the end of what was an otherwise healing and productive meeting last November, the Bishop himself asked what else I would like for him/his office to do on my behalf. I said that I would like for Dorsch to write a letter to me. I did not mention anything about a letter to my family. I'm blessed to have two brothers who've taken your office up on its ministry, but their letters are separate and distinct from mine. Do you really not see this distinction?

In my meeting, I went on to explain that an apology letter from Dorsch would connect him with reflecting on the crimes he committed against me. I went further to share with the bishop and you and the priest in attendance that writing has an emotionally healing aspect to me. The fact that Dorsch wrote the letter, in which he does not deny and yet like other abusers claims that he "never intended" any harm to me, is itself an admission that lots of bad stuff happened. He now knows that I know how very bad it was, and yet he himself clearly feels that he was doing good. Well, let's keep it a bit more real as adults . . . buying a kid an ice cream cone is a good thing, but then having an 11-year-old suck your 38-year-old penis is not (Dorsch and I are 27 years apart!). In fact, it's a crime. The list of incidents I'll spare you, but I mention this one because I do have a good memory of what I told you and yours there at your office that Saturday following Thanksgiving.

Rita, your letter of apology falls short. Your colleagues and the Bishop/whomever else on his staff that had the Dorsch letter vetted owe me apologies for bungling this development. Also, I don't want it to get lost in the shuffle that confident advisers here have seen the letter and, in their professional experience, are most confident that Church lawyers advised on its construction. It's not for me to say, since He Alone upstairs is always watching. However, I'm only human and do express now how most ashamed I am yet again for how your office's veil of secrecy has brought shame to the Catholic institution of faith. I'm determined to have a sequel to the current hit movie DOUBT made—its working title is SHAME!

My therapist and psychiatrist are most concerned about my healing and recovery, which have been dealt a blow by the way you and your staff there have mishandled this particular request.

God's peace to your office.

The Perpetrator: Richard J. Dorsch

Michael's poem below more accurately and succinctly summarizes the abuse that took place—the perpetrator's analysis was clearly still a bit rosier than the harsh reality that had taken place.

Cause/Effect/Conclusion–
Victim/Survivor/Liver.
Or, No More Liver Damage!
By Michael Unglo, November 1, 2009.

It—sodomy—was in the rectory,
As well as—masturbation—in the confessional.
To wit this is a perverse life story.
It's about sex by force, love lost to the professorial.

His abuser was priestly and diabolical.
He was the victim—ages 10, 11, 12, 13, 14—
In search of mere protection, nothing astronomical,
He sought. Spent, he ran from every vile, cruel scene.

Victims live on a prayer or two. No! More!
This survivor instead chose to be just.
He became a guy striving forward for what's in store—
Living, smiling, being, and giving his best.

His Christian name is Michael,
His last name could just as well be yours.
The abuse was part of a Catholic cycle
Akin to doing Saturday's household chores.

In grade school his marks were low.
In high school his letter grades topped!
By college he was giving great blow
Jobs. He worked, studied, and binged, then stopped.

His first real job was that of an editor.
He then came out and found a boyfriend.
His next job took him to the Big Apple as a writer.
There he worked, drank, and sexed it up, before it came to an end.

In a flash, mind taken back to that kneeler in the sacristy
At All Saints Roman Catholic Church in Etna, Pennsylvania,
He downed a bottle of pills. In a fit of blasphemy
He reached for cutlery and cut his neck as if back in Transylvania.

His last name in Italian originally meant 'the Hungarian'
Before it was bastardized officially at the Port of New York.
A second suicide attempt required a pharmaceutical armamentarium,
Reining in the psychosis. His diagnosis now has him living like a dork.

Michael graduated with honors from the University of Pennsylvania and became a successful marketing executive in New York City before his world came crashing down from the scars of child sex abuse. He died living in a mental-healthcare facility, for which the diocese of Pittsburgh would no longer pay, despite authorizing and paying for such care initially. It is hard to live on top of the world, academically and professionally, and then be knocked down by flashbacks and C-PTSD originating from when you were ten years old. Once down again, he was then kicked again—in the form of the full and final release request—by the very institution that brought him harm in the first place.

Why priests can't marry by the way—yet another decision by the catholic church to grow and protect their financial coffers

A great article on this topic is from *The Economist*.

The Perpetrator: Richard J. Dorsch

"Why Catholic priests practice celibacy: The rules date from the Middle Ages"
March 23, 2017
By M.H.

In an interview with a German magazine earlier this month, Pope Francis suggested that he would be open to the idea of allowing married men to become priests. Such a change, though momentous, would be a return to, rather than a break from, early Christian tradition: nowhere does the New Testament explicitly require priests to be celibate. For the first thousand years of Christianity, it was not uncommon for priests to have families. The first pope, St. Peter, was a married man; many early popes had children. How did celibacy become part of the Catholic tradition?

Celibacy is one of the biggest acts of self-sacrifice a Catholic priest is called upon to make, forgoing spouse, progeny, and sexual fulfillment for his relationship with parishioners and God. According to the Catholic Church's Code of Canon Law, celibacy is a "special gift of God" which allows practitioners to follow more closely the example of Christ, who was chaste. Another reason is that when a priest enters into service to God, the church becomes his highest calling. If he were to have a family, there would be the potential for conflict between his spiritual and familial duties. The Vatican regards it as being easier for unattached men to commit to the church, as they have more time for devotion and fewer distractions.

The earliest written reference to celibacy comes from 305 AD at the Spanish Council of Elvira, a local assembly of clergymen who met to discuss matters pertaining to the church. Canon 33 forbids clerics in the church—bishops, priests, and deacons—from having sexual relations with their wives and from having children, though not from entering into marriage. It was not until ecumenical meetings of the Catholic Church at the First and Second Lateran councils in 1123 and 1139 that priests were explicitly forbidden from marrying. *Eliminating the prospect of marriage had the added benefit of ensuring that children or wives of priests did not make claims on property acquired throughout a priest's life, which thus could be retained by the church.* It took centuries for the practice of celibacy to become widespread, but it eventually became the norm in the Western Catholic church.

Despite the decrees from the Middle Ages, celibacy is still a "discipline" of the church, which can be changed, rather than a "dogma," or a divinely revealed truth from God which cannot be altered. As the world has changed, the Church has had a harder time recruiting priests. Numbers have been dropping: between 1970 and 2014, the world's Catholic population grew from 654m to 1.23bn, while the number of priests declined from 420,000 to 414,000. Some prospective priests don't want to choose between having a life with God and having a family. It is not inconceivable that the time will come again when they can have both.

So, there you have it. The catholic church's unreasonable and unhealthy stance on sexuality, marriage, and priesthood led to recruiting many dysfunctional and confused men who found sanctuary in an institution while they practiced their pedophilia and other sexual abuse. But, hey, they deepened their assets along the way—their primary aim with the practice.

11

Correspondence with the diocese of Pittsburgh RE: Support of and for Michael

In this chapter, I present further detail around communications between our family and the diocese of Pittsburgh staff, including the bishop, so that everyone can see for themselves the content of those documents and how they treat victims of child sex abuse versus their own perpetrators of that crime.

Throughout Michael's journey after his first suicide attempt, the diocese of Pittsburgh made it clear that they wanted to limit their financial exposure in the matter, and they were always looking for an exit strategy so that they could cease funding and helping him to recover. They set their own arbitrary timeline for Michael's healing. Yet, they never stopped providing for the financial well-being of the perpetrator, Richard J. Dorsch. Bishop Zubik, in a meeting with Rita E. Flaherty, Paul, and me on December 6, 2008, admitted that the diocese was still funding Dorsch's ongoing living expenses with a monthly check. They were doing this despite the fact that Dorsch was convicted of crimes against children in 1995. More than 13 years after Dorsch's conviction, the diocese was still providing for Dorsch's care. Yet, the diocese and catholic church at large balk at helping victims and want to set their own timelines for how quickly victims should heal.

TO: Sam Unglo
FROM: Mrs. Rita E. Flaherty, M.S.W., L.S.W.—Diocesan Assistance Coordinator
DATE: July 15, 2009

> I'm sure that there is a sense of relief for you and your family to know that Michael is now at Sheppard Pratt. Based on what I have read, Sheppard Pratt seems to have a very comprehensive treatment program that will hopefully assist Michael in his healing and recovery. I am in the process of arranging payment to the "The Retreat" Program in the event that Michael will eventually be able to enter that program following his in-patient stay. It is my understanding after speaking with Mr. Lois Turner-Feig, LCSW-C that this payment will be refunded to the Diocese of Pittsburgh if this type of care is not deemed to be appropriate for Michael's needs.
>
> For the sake of clarity, I want to outline for you and your family that the Diocese of Pittsburgh has agreed to provide for coverage of The Retreat at Sheppard Pratt for a 30-day period. Payment for the initial 20 days will be sent out soon, as is required by Sheppard Pratt. I'm sure they will notify us when the remainder of the cost is due. Over and above that, the diocese has agreed to cover the cost of your sister, Frances, to travel to New York to accompany Michael to Sheppard Pratt. Obviously, her travel back to Pittsburgh is covered as well. In addition, yesterday we agreed to cover the cost of the ambulance transport for Michael

Correspondence with the diocese of Pittsburgh . . .

from Bellevue to Sheppard Pratt if this expense is not covered by Michael's insurance.

If you have read through the Resident Agreement for The Retreat Program at Sheppard Pratt, you will see that there is a list of incidental costs that may be incurred by the resident over and above the per diem rate. These costs include such things as personal entertainment, dry cleaning, salon services, dental care, etc. Coverage for those things itemized in the Resident Agreement is not part of our agreement with Sheppard Pratt. The diocese is unable to cover these additional costs. The one exception would be our coverage for TMS (Transcranial Magnetic Stimulation) if that procedure became necessary. I share all of this with you so that there is no misunderstanding about what the diocese is and is not able to cover.

While it is certainly our desire to be of as much assistance as possible to Michael, your family and other families and victims of abuse, by necessity there must be limitations. I hope that you and the rest of the Unglo family have seen thus far that the Diocese of Pittsburgh is concerned about Michael's well-being. It is our desire to help him to the fullest extent of our limited resources. Please know that all of you are in my prayers. I will continue to be here to support you to the best of my ability.

The diocese forced Michael to move from place to place due to financial concerns. Michael was doing well at Sheppard Pratt, but it was too expensive for the diocese's tastes, and they insisted that he be transferred elsewhere, which was ultimately to Austen Riggs Center in Stockbridge, Massachusetts.

The Murder of Innocence

TO: Rita Flaherty, LCSW-C—Diocese of Pittsburgh
FROM: Donald Ross, M.D., Medical Director, The Retreat at Sheppard Pratt
DATE: September 4, 2009

It is my understanding that you are the social worker with the Diocese of Pittsburgh who has been facilitating authorization and payment for Michael Unglo's care. This letter is in follow-up to the Diocese's request to receive an update on Michael's diagnosis and prognosis given its reimbursements to date for Michael's care.

In my professional opinion, Michael continues to suffer from a complex post-traumatic stress disorder (PTSD) and has only recently recovered from a psychotic episode, which was related to his PTSD. This and his related symptoms of depression are clearly linked to the sexual abuse that Michael has described that he suffered at the hands of Richard Dorsch, then priest, from 1981 through 1985.

It is not uncommon for sex abuse victims to function relatively normally for years and then to have an upsurge of PTSD symptoms, even to the point of a psychotic break, as has been with the case with Michael.

Michael's recovery has progressed slowly, and he will continue to need care for quite some time. While progress continues to be made, Michael is in a depression right now and at high risk for relapse. It is not possible to provide an exact timeline of when full-time care would cease. His safety outside of a structured therapeutic environment is a significant concern.

Correspondence with the diocese of Pittsburgh . . .

My recommendation, along with Michael's agreement at this point, is that he continues in a longer term, full-time psychiatric care program after he departs The Retreat at Sheppard Pratt. Making those arrangements will take some time, and will require a financial commitment for his care. The program needs to be clinically appropriate and acceptable to Michael, and Michael needs to be well enough to move to such a program. Once there, it is my estimate that Michael will require three to six months in this facility based on the nature of the program and Michael's current state.

Please let me know if you require any additional information to authorize payment for Michael's continued care. Michael and his family appreciate the Diocese's continued support to work toward healing, and it is my hope that Michael will continue to move forward and make progress.

TO: Rita Flaherty, LCSW-C—Diocese of Pittsburgh
FROM: Donald Ross, M.D., Medical Director, The Retreat at Sheppard Pratt
DATE: September 25, 2009

As an essential part of our treatment of Michael Unglo, we are in the process of seeking the right placement once he is ready for discharge from The Retreat (in approximately two weeks). Our clinical recommendation is that he transfers to the program at Austen Riggs, which has the right combination of therapeutic engagement, clinical supervision, and ability to help Michael take the next steps as he progresses towards outpatient status. A less restrictive environment in the immediate future would make a successful outcome less likely and trigger safety concerns. Michael has thought through his options along with us, and he is amenable to transferring to Austen Riggs.

The cost of Austen Riggs is $1,065 per day for an initial six-week period, which encompasses their highest level of care and is required for Michael at this point in time. The total cost for that period is $44,730. Austen Riggs is capable of providing less supervised care at less cost per day after that time if it is indicated.

It is my medical opinion that Michael needs this level of care as his next step towards recovery from his complex post-traumatic stress disorder and the aftermath of his most recent suicide attempt. I hope the Diocese will be able to support this financially.

TO: bishop David A. Zubik
CC: Michael R. Unglo, Renee Unglo, Anna U. Dzikowski, Paul M. Unglo II, Frances M. Samber
FROM: Sam Unglo
DATE: November 1, 2009

This letter is to set the record straight as my brother, Michael R. Unglo, settles in at Austen Riggs to receive essential care for his chronic post-traumatic stress disorder (PTSD). Your subordinate, William G. Batz, wrote a most disturbing email dated October 9, 2009, in which he claimed that your office will not be providing necessary supports for Michael as he moves forward living outside of mental-healthcare facilities. The letter suggested that the diocese will provide no additional support to Michael. I am sure you know

Correspondence with the diocese of Pittsburgh . . .

its contents already, but if not, I am including a copy for you. He included Rita E. Flaherty, Rita F. Joyce, and Frederick P. O'Brien, the last two of whom I have never met, spoken to, or been in communication with.

Let me preface the balance of this letter by saying that I write on behalf of Michael. Throughout this process, I think some at the diocesan office have lost sight of whose best interests really need to be kept center stage here—the victim's; he is the one trying to recover.

Batz's message that the diocesan office will sever its obligations to Michael by paying only for his expenses at Austen Riggs misses the mark wildly and ignores the facts of Michael's case. Following Michael's first suicide attempt in June 2008, due to what Richard J. Dorsch, now ex-priest and convicted child molester, inflicted on him, when Michael found his way to your office by way of the Survivors Network of those Abused by Priests (SNAP), it was suggested to Michael that a timeline of up to a year of reimbursed medical expenses would be imposed. Even then, Michael made it known to Flaherty that no such willy-nilly and arbitrary expectation for his recovery would be tolerated by him. Michael dug deep and proceeded with intensive outpatient therapy for months, and that helped to anchor him. He even found firm footing again in the aftermath of his job loss in October 2008, landing an opportunity that allowed him to earn $125 per hour on a freelance basis. I mention this because it is important that you understand what has been lost during the course of this year due to a second suicide attempt that my brother endured in June 2009 because of what Dorsch inflicted on him. Chronic PTSD is a lifelong condition, and you and the diocesan office should keep that in mind as Michael seeks firm financial footing even as he copes at Austen Riggs. For the record, my brother vomited while at Sheppard Pratt when told of your office's attempt to pay out a lump sum of $250,000 and be done.

That said, please allow me to be very candid with some thoughts for you to consider and reflect upon.

The diocese did nothing for my brother until 2008. Dorsch sexually abused Michael by forcing hand jobs, oral sex, and anal sex on a regular basis over the course of five years! This is to make it explicitly clear so that your office comprehends the damage and extreme nature of the flashbacks that have resulted in my brother's chronic PTSD, which is at the core of both of Michael's suicide attempts.

Since 1981, it is my estimate that the diocese has paid Dorsch about $20,000 a year in living expenses and ongoing support. You have no problem supporting the perpetrator. The current value of $20,000 from 1981 to 2009 using a 10% investment rate is $2,972,618.59. One could easily argue that you have a moral obligation to pay Michael that same amount. After all, he is the victim, not Dorsch. Let me state that again: Michael is the victim, not Dorsch. I am still not convinced the diocese gets that.

I can understand the diocese does not want an indefinite timeline of requests from Michael or my family with respect to costs. Every time we make a request, the diocese seems to undermine the dignity and honesty of our requests, which are simply asking for what is fair and right. I, as always, am making myself available on Michael's behalf to talk with you about settling on a final payout that is separate and distinct from Michael's expenses at Austen Riggs. You need to understand that, as Michael bravely works at his recovery, the toll

Correspondence with the diocese of Pittsburgh . . .

it has taken on him extends beyond mere medical bills. A final payout amount must be decided upon and extended to Michael in the near term, precisely because his medical condition has bled him dry due to lost income and compromised his qualifications to secure housing. Michael has his life to continue outside the walls of medical facilities. Glaringly and painfully real each and every day to him is his homelessness. I trust that Batz was just ignorant of that fact when he wrote his email.

Michael has asked further for me to communicate to you that job opportunities to make in excess of $180,000 a year have been presented to him as recently as the past month. Because Michael has his dignity intact and is clearly committed to his long-term recovery, he is not compromising his care for just another six-figure salary or an inadequate lump sum of $250,000 that was suggested by your office in the recent past. Contrary to Batz's suggestion that your willingness to live up to your responsibilities has run out, doing what is fair and right for Michael remains to be done.

If the diocese thinks that it will not pay anything additionally or participate further in talks, please know that there are other means my family will consider and has already been in preliminary discussions about, including having Michael's story with that of the diocese told on local and national news agencies. Surely, the diocese does not want to relive the mess of the 1990s and earlier this decade (for example, having it broadcast that you still financially support convicted child molesters). This is not a threat. To use a line from Batz's email, I simply want the diocese to know how we will react formally to Batz's statement, "We want you and your family to know that this will be the limit of our willingness to provide assistance."

Your willingness? The church created this mess, and you, as bishop, have every moral obligation to make things right.

And let us talk more about Dorsch's damage. Are you aware that there are many other boys from All Saints parish in Etna, Pennsylvania, who were also altar boys with Michael who have already committed suicide? You may say that you are unaware or that it is coincidental. And, in the end, God knows the truth. How do you sleep at night knowing the church has not righted the wrongs of priests who sexually abused innocent and God-fearing children? Children are taught to love and respect God, and priests preyed on this very understanding of children to have sex with them. Those children, now adults, struggle every single day to move forward despite troubling and painful flashbacks to scenes when their childhood innocence was violently destroyed.

I also want to address your disposition that the church acted correctly throughout everything with Dorsch. Any institution that allows for an environment where a priest sexually abuses hundreds of children over a 25- to 30-year period is a failure. I do not care if no one supposedly knew about it until the mid-1990s. The structure of the institution allowed it to happen for 25 to 30 years, and that in and of itself is negligence and an inexcusable failure.

Bishops are powerful people and should be able to bring about what they think is right. Words and apology masses are not enough. Taking care of the victims is the action that needs to stand behind the words. The second reading, on September 13, 2009, spoke about how words are not enough to live out faith; actions are what tell the true story. The diocese needs to live the words of the gospel.

Correspondence with the diocese of Pittsburgh . . .

For your reference, here is the second reading from September 13, 2009.

> Reading II
> James 2:14-18
>
>> What good is it, my brothers and sisters,
>> if someone says he has faith but does not have works?
>> Can that faith save him?
>> If a brother or sister has nothing to wear
>> and has no food for the day,
>> and one of you says to them,
>> "Go in peace, keep warm, and eat well,"
>> but you do not give them the necessities of the body,
>> what good is it?
>> So also faith of itself,
>> if it does not have works, is dead.
>>
>> Indeed someone might say,
>> "You have faith and I have works."
>> Demonstrate your faith to me without works,
>> and I will demonstrate my faith to you from my works.

Most of my thoughts on this whole subject occur in church and are inspired by God. I believe He has granted me courage to articulate what needs to be said and what you need to hear. Some of what I am saying you may not want to hear, but I think you need to hear it. You are in the position to make things right. At the end of the day, bishop, I am a fair man and simply want fairness to be achieved on this issue. You sat with me and my brother Paul, looked us straight in the eye on December 6, 2008, and told us you would do whatever it takes to right the wrong that was done to our brother by one of the church's own. Now, I get a letter from one of your subordinates telling me it is all over. I do not think that is how a man of God honors his word.

Your and the diocesan office's disposition to date on living expenses and matters financial other than mental healthcare has been illogical. Michael finds himself in financial distress because of the fallout from the graphic hand jobs, oral sex, and anal sex he was forced to provide to Dorsch. The diocese has every moral obligation to help Michael land on his feet financially after Austen Riggs so he can begin living a real life once again outside the walls of mental-healthcare facilities. And, if you ask again if the church should do this for all other victims, indeed it should. If the church is that financially strapped, it can stop paying for the care of all the damn child molesters who used to be priests.

As an objective point of reference, one of Michael's treating physicians at Sheppard Pratt has attested that the Archdiocese of Boston has provided support and final payouts over and above mental-healthcare expenses for other victims. Additionally, as recently as this past week, the diocese of Savannah has agreed to pay more than $4 million to a victim of sexual abuse at the hands of a priest (please see enclosed article); again, to provide support beyond just mental-healthcare expenses. Michael's teams of experts are as concerned as he is about the other aspects of his life, which are in ruins because of the damages exacted on Michael by Dorsch. I have faith that you will remind your subordinates at the diocesan office to consider the totality of my brother and not reduce him to the mental illness against which he bravely battles each and every day, and has battled now for 28 years. Michael is broken in the most extreme way, and you have an

Correspondence with the diocese of Pittsburgh . . .

obligation to help ensure his ability to move forward as a citizen of the world.

Long are all of our roads, and yet for some of us the road is longer still. Michael has the added burden—the mental agony and long-term anguish caused by years of violent sexual abuse at the hands of a priest—placed upon him that he continues to carry and try to fight through. Again, Michael asked nothing of the church from 1981 through 2008. He continues to fight to be a survivor. The church should be looking for ways to embrace him, not for ways to draw lines in the sand and write off any future obligation and somehow proclaim that Austen Riggs is it and that it better provide a "salutary" outcome.

Bishop, you yourself have spoken of healing, and you must agree that healing does not have a predetermined timeframe. It occurs over time, and the victim must heal—not be forced to heal because of arbitrary and unrealistic time pressures imposed by the very institution that failed him. What would Jesus do? I strongly suggest you reflect on this, perhaps more than anything else in the letter. Surely, you do not want the media to portray you as having failed a victim of sexual abuse at the hands of a priest, when so many others have already committed suicide.

The diocese's current stance of wishing for a "salutary" outcome and providing for nothing else is not acceptable. It needs to do more to provide for a solid financial foundation on which Michael can build a real future. You cannot just cut off support for Michael and hope for the best. That solid foundation is needed now as Michael's finances have been devastated by the fallout from the Dorsch abuse.

Chronic PTSD is a lifelong, destabilizing condition. It is not like an illness that has a discrete cure. In fact, Michael has worked hard to resolve his psychotic depression since arriving at Sheppard Pratt and no longer needs to take medications. The psychotic depression is a symptom of the chronic PTSD. I trust you understand the difference. In Michael's case, that chronic PTSD has its origins in the repeated sexual abuse exacted by a priest, Richard J. Dorsch, of the diocese of Pittsburgh, and the diocese continues to care for Dorsch. For Michael, there is no end date to his chronic PTSD. Again, it is not like an illness that has a discrete cure. The diocese must provide some payout that allows for the hope of continued healing and recovering. The lump-sum payout needs to recognize the value of his accomplishments to date and present opportunities, as well as allow for him to maintain hope in the face of inevitable flare-ups of his lifelong battle in the coming years.

Your office must rise to the occasion now, as Michael works to step down from Austen Riggs on sure footing, so that with peace of mind, he will move forward and show family and friends alike his essential enthusiasm for living that enabled him to climb a mountain in the first place. As Michael's illness has exacted far more damage than just medical and psychological tolls, I trust you recognize how foolhardy and catastrophic it appears to help someone down a cliff only to leave him stranded at the base. Now is the time for us to discuss a fair and reality-based resolution.

Bishop, I sincerely hope that you treat this as an opportunity to respond appropriately and to help save and rescue a victim of sexual abuse at the hands of a priest. There have been many victims whom the church has not helped before those victims

Correspondence with the diocese of Pittsburgh . . .

committed suicide from the pain caused by their abuse. You have the opportunity to help a victim reach full recovery. Please do not stop in the middle of the journey and induce more stress on my brother—stress that may cause him to consider additional self-harming acts.

I look forward to talking to you and expect a call no later than Wednesday, November 11, 2009.

TO: Unglo, Samuel J
CC: Flaherty, Rita E; Joyce, Rita F; O'Brien, Frederick P
FROM: Batz, William G.
DATE: Friday, October 09, 2009, 12:52 PM
SUBJECT: RE: M. Unglo

The diocese intended to pay for Michael's care at Sheppard Pratt through October 7, 2009. Under the circumstances of Michael's admission to Austen Riggs on Thursday, October 15th, the diocese will pay the fees at Sheppard Pratt until his day of discharge there on Wednesday, October 14th. There seems no point now in disrupting Michael's living arrangements during these last few days. Although this exceeds our original understanding, we are sensitive to Dr. Ross' recommendation in the matter.

Please allow me to enumerate the diocese's plan going forward. I do this so that you and your family will have a clear understanding of what the diocese has or has not volunteered to do after Michael's discharge from Sheppard Pratt.

The diocese will pay for Michael's continued care at Austen Riggs for a period of six months. We are prepared shortly to send $42,000 to Austen

```
Riggs, which is the required down payment prior
to Michael's admission.

On the matter of transition, travel to Stockbridge,
MA, etc., we will reimburse travel costs for Michael
and family members accompanying him up to a limit
of $1,000.

Beyond these expenditures, which are considerable,
the diocese does not have future resources to make
available. We want you and your family to know
that this will be the limit of our willingness to
provide assistance.

With the extensive care that Michael has and will
continue to receive, we sincerely hope he will be
able to experience a salutary outcome to his recent
episode of illness.
```

Diocese to Pay $4M for Abuse

BY **DANA CLARK FELTY**

Posted Oct. 29, 2009, at 12:16 AM

The Catholic Diocese of Savannah has agreed to pay more than $4 million to the alleged victim of an abusive former priest in order to avoid going to trial.

The Diocese released a statement Wednesday afternoon announcing the $4.24 million agreement reached with former St. James Catholic School student Allan Ranta Jr.

Ranta had filed a complaint in a Jasper County, S.C., civil court stating he was molested from 1978 to 1983, starting when he was 10 years old, by former priest Wayland Y. Brown.

Correspondence with the diocese of Pittsburgh . . .

Ranta claimed former Savannah Bishop Raymond Lessard and other diocesan officials knew Brown posed a danger to children but failed to take action.

Brown, 66, was convicted in 2003 of sexually abusing two Maryland boys, ages 12 and 13, in 1974. He was released from prison in April 2008 after serving half of his sentence and now is listed on the Maryland Sex Offender Registry as living in Baltimore.

Ranta's attorney, Larry Richter, described the settlement as "giant" but appropriate considering the type of abuse involved and the degree to which he says diocesan officials ignored warning signs.

Richter said the settlement doesn't include $200,000 already paid to Ranta for medical treatment relating to the alleged abuse.

In the diocese's written statement, Savannah Bishop J. Kevin Boland apologized.

"I am sorry for all the pain and suffering experienced by Mr. Ranta, and my prayers go out not only to him, but to all victims of child sexual abuse that each may find the healing they seek," Boland said in the statement posted on the diocese's Web site.

Richter described Boland's apology as "insufficient."

"We call on Bishop (J.) Kevin Boland and all bishops to identify publicly known abuser priests," Richter said. "We repeatedly called on (the Charleston) diocese to do it. Of course, it didn't. And we've called repeatedly on the Diocese of Savannah to make such identifications, and that hasn't happened either."

Based in Mount Pleasant, S.C., Richter won a $12 million class-action settlement against the Catholic Diocese of Charleston in 2007.

The settlement with Ranta releases the Savannah diocese, Lessard, and Boland as parties to the lawsuit. Ranta will continue his civil case against Brown, Richter said. A hearing is scheduled for December 7.

Jeff Anderson, a St. Paul, Minn., attorney who has represented hundreds of victims across the U.S. for 25 years, said the Savannah diocese's settlement represents the second-largest payout to an individual in the history of the priest sex abuse scandal.

"It demonstrates that the liability and the legal responsibility of the Diocese of Savannah and its officials was extraordinarily aggravated," Anderson said.

The largest individual payout to date came in 2001, when two California dioceses agreed to pay $5.2 million to Ryan DiMaria, a man who claimed he had been sexually abused as a teenager by a priest at a church high school.

Victim advocates said the settlement is bittersweet.

"For every individual survivor, a settlement does in fact represent a hard-earned, long-overdue validation and closure," said David Clohessy, national director of the Survivors Network of those Abused by Priests.

"In the larger context, though, every settlement also represents a victory for bishops who want to continue to hide the truth. There's no denying that more cover-up by the hierarchy is exposed when cases go to trial."

The Savannah diocese says since 2002, it has provided "safe-environment training" to volunteers and staff who work with children and has hired an independent auditing agency to review practices relating to the protection of children.

Until Wednesday, the diocese had paid about $400,000 for various types of treatments for victims of sexual abuse, said spokeswoman Barbara King.

While I included the newspaper article as an enclosure to my letter to bishop Zubik on November 1, 2009, as an example of a diocese paying a significant sum outright to a victim, the article also makes a very important point: That settlements by the catholic church simply hide the untold truth. I have spent so many hours ensuring that this book would be published for all those to read who want to see how the catholic church really acts in these horrific situations.

Correspondence with the diocese of Pittsburgh . . .

The following is the response of the diocese to my letter of November 1, 2009.

TO: Sam Unglo
FROM: William G. Batz, Ph.D., General Secretary, Diocese of Pittsburgh
DATE: November 10, 2009

We received your package and letter dated November 1, 2009. As I mentioned in my email yesterday, the Bishop is unavailable to place the phone call on Wednesday, which you demanded. We intend this letter instead to be our response to the topics you raised.

Underlying your long discourse there are certain assumptions and expectations. Some we share. Just like you, for example, we earnestly hope that your brother Michael will be able to leave Austen Riggs and move forward as "a citizen of the world," to borrow your term. We pray that Michael will leave treatment with the ability to resume his life as an independent, self-sufficient person.

That being said, you seem to assume that the Diocese of Pittsburgh is somehow liable or obligated to pay for Michael's indefinite care. In good faith and without any legal obligation, the Diocese volunteered to cover the cost of premium residential care at some of the country's costliest psychiatric facilities which you proposed. Still, the Diocese is not liable for the perpetrator's conduct. It has conducted itself properly and responsibly in handling this case. There was never any improper action on the part of the Diocese which would remotely create a legal obligation to provide such assistance, certainly not to the degree already provided, or which you seem to demand. We need to state clearly that our assistance is an act of compassion and concern for your brother, but not an obligation.

You have also demanded, in effect, that the Diocese provide assistance in unlimited amounts, for any and all expenses, for an indefinite period of time. You have alluded to unrelated cases elsewhere (e.g., Savannah), in a manner which intimates that something similar will occur here. In addition to the generous support we have supplied so far, we have stated that we will enable Michael to receive extended treatment at Austen Riggs for six months, but that will finally be the limit of our assistance. It is important to recognize that the Diocese has no plans for any further payments for any purpose beyond the current course of treatment.

Your letter exudes a demanding and adversarial tone. You indicate that there are other alternatives you may pursue if your assertive expectations are not met. We do not seek an adversarial relationship with you. Our intent has been to help Michael to the extent we can do so, while exercising good stewardship over the resources entrusted to the Church for the benefits of all people. In other words, we cannot responsibly volunteer to commit limitless amounts to any one cause, regardless of our sincere, good faith intent to help as much as we can.

We respect your dedication to your brother, and we understand that you may not be satisfied with anything short of unlimited financial assistance. Our goal is to provide help and support to Michael in recovery from his recent episode within the limits of prudent use of Church resources. Based on the

Correspondence with the diocese of Pittsburgh . . .

tone of your letter, we will have to live with the consequences of this disagreement.

Some time ago, you asked that we use you, Sam, as the sole contact point for Michael and your family. Now we would ask the reciprocal favor. In the future, kindly refer all correspondence to the Diocese through me and my office as General Secretary of the Diocese.

I am sorry that our conversation has taken on an adversarial dimension, but that does not keep us from praying and hoping with you for Michael's health and improvement.

What I find truly fascinating about Batz's letter is his line, "Our intent has been to help Michael to the extent we can do so, while exercising good stewardship over the resources entrusted to the Church for the benefits of all people." The diocese of Pittsburgh continues to pay for the living expenses of a convicted child molester to this day, yet they place limits on helping the victims of that perpetrator. By paying for the perpetrator to live, does that not require them to pay for the victims' care indefinitely? The hypocrisy of the roman catholic church lives on!

Additionally, Batz's letter took a noticeably legal tone: "That being said, you seem to assume that the Diocese of Pittsburgh is somehow liable or obligated to pay for Michael's indefinite care. In good faith and without any legal obligation, the Diocese volunteered to cover the cost of premium residential care at some of the country's costliest psychiatric facilities which you proposed. Still, the Diocese is not liable for the perpetrator's conduct." The catholic church has gone out of its way to protect itself legally. It saw itself as legally not having to provide for my brother's care, yet it continues to fund the perpetrator to this day. Does it not have a moral obligation to provide for victims of child sex abuse at its hands? After all, it is a religious organization that supposedly holds itself to a moral standard that God would be proud of, not only to a legal standard that might be incorrect or currently unjustly prevailing, due to an ill-conceived statute of limitations lobbied for to protect the guilty.

I subsequently wrote bishop Zubik letting him know my disappointment at his distancing himself from seeing to it that my brother was cared for appropriately. He wrote the following letter and would have no further contact with us until Michael's third and final suicide attempt on May 4, 2010.

TO: Sam Unglo
CC: William G. Batz, Ph.D.
FROM: bishop David A. Zubik
DATE: December 21, 2009

On December 2, 2009, you shared an email in which you expressed your disappointment with me that I did not personally reply to your earlier letter of November 1, 2009, about the ongoing care of your dear brother, Michael.

It was my hope that the letter from Dr. Bill Batz, dated November 10, 2009, showed the ongoing concern of the Diocese of Pittsburgh for your brother's healing at Austen Riggs.

To simplify all matters, just as you requested that all communications about Michael from the Diocese be done through you, I thought it simpler that all communications with the Diocese be done through Dr. Batz.

Please know just as the Diocese has responded to Michael's healing, I continue to pray for you, Michael, and all of your family.

Correspondence with the diocese of Pittsburgh . . .

```
With every best wish for a blessed Christmas and
a grace-filled 2010, I remain

Your brother in Christ,
Most Reverend David A. Zubik
Bishop of Pittsburgh
```

Zubik hid behind prayer and supposed holiness while what the diocese actually did was to abandon my brother at his greatest hour of need.

Things would spiral further in the following few months. It would become clear that Michael would become more vulnerable and needed more time to heal, but the diocese would not listen and would still send him a Full and Final Release (as covered earlier), despite knowing the circumstances under which he was suffering.

Great Barrington Police Dept. Voluntary Statement
465 Main Street, Great Barrington, MA 01230

Date: Thursday, March 25, 2010
Place: Great Barrington Police Dept.
Person Giving Statement: Michael R. Unglo
DOB: 04-11-1971. POB: Pittsburgh, PA.
Address: 25 Main St., Stockbridge, MA 01262
Time Started: 1330 Hrs. Time Ended: 1405 Hrs.
Number of Pages: 2
Interviewing Officer(s): Officer Zucco
Case #: 10-59-OF / 10-69-AC

The Murder of Innocence

My name is Michael R. Unglo, and I am here to give a statement about a motor vehicle accident that happened last night with my friend Julia Berkman in Great Barrington. Last night at approximately 8:57 PM, Julia and I were coming back from dinner. We had dinner at Koi restaurant in Great Barrington. While at the restaurant, Julia and I did not drink any alcoholic beverages. As we were traveling northbound on Rt. 7, we were somewhere in the middle between K-Mart shopping center and that garage that is located at the foot of the hill. At this time, I noticed a body come from the southbound lane. I could not give you a description of the body other than knowing it was human. The body was low to the ground and in the diving position (head first). As the body hit the front of the car, it was still in motion, causing it to go underneath the car. Before the body dove under the car, there was no time for me or Julia to yell or do anything until after the impact. We both started screaming after the impact while the body was still under the car. Julia then hit the brakes to slow down while the body was still under the vehicle. At that point both the driver's-side and passenger-side airbags deployed. We were both wearing our seat belts that were a shoulder and lap belt combination. The car had slowed down, but Julia was no longer in control of the vehicle. I kept telling Julia that we had to get out of the vehicle. The car had slowed down significantly enough to where we could get out even though it was still moving. We then got out of the car while it was still traveling down the northbound lane. The car continued to travel down the northbound lane and then eventually drifted off to the northbound shoulder and hit the guard rail. Once out of the car, I dialed 911 from the side of the road. Julia then met me on the side of the road while I was talking with the 911 dispatch. I did my best to give the dispatch all the information that they needed. As I was talking to 911 dispatch, another witness came over, and I offered dispatch to speak with this witness to get more information about the person who had been hit. This witness then brought my phone back and tried to calm Julia and me down. He encouraged us to stay by our

Correspondence with the diocese of Pittsburgh . . .

car and again tried to calm us down. The police came very quickly and tended to the accident scene while gathering our information. At this time, I was on the phone with Riggs talking to friends and a nurse about the accident and being shook up. While waiting for the police to do their initial investigation, some of my friends from Riggs showed up and were allowed to pull off the side of the road north of the accident scene. Julia and I then sat with them in the car because it was getting cold out. I expressed concern to the police about wanting to get back to Riggs. The police then finished taking our information and phone numbers and told us they would contact us for statements later.

The following two updates, one dated April 26, 2010, and the other dated May 3, 2010 (a day before Michael died), provide a window into his state of mind and the stress he was under given the trauma and stress from the car accident and knowing that the diocese of Pittsburgh had put a Full and Final Release in his hands:

Medication Progress Note—Austen Riggs, Stockbridge, MA—April 26, 2010

> Michael reports feeling a complicated range of symptoms. He is experiencing PTSD symptoms from his car accident, which occurred exactly a month ago. He is having flashbacks and intrusive thoughts about this. There is some overlap and reinforcing of his sexual abuse trauma because he says, "Both happened in a car." He is having flashbacks and intrusive thoughts of his past sexual abuse and things that were said to him during those incidents, as well as things former lovers have said to him and things the police said to him (in the past when he had decompensated and the police were rescuing him and/or taking him to the hospital).

He recognizes that the fact that he had to interface with the police in the context of the car accident is likely triggering these memories. He is feeling more depressed and is concerned about this—he says he is noticing decreased motivation, decreased social environment, decreased interest in doing things—a sense of things taking more effort, increased napping, and generally beginning to shut down. He wants to live and is future-oriented, with no expression of suicidal ideation.

We reviewed the stressors he's been dealing with in the last 4-6 weeks, the increased (and addition of) PTSD symptoms, related to both his recent trauma and past traumas and the way some of these PTSD symptoms, particularly memories of having hurtful things said to him (which he experiences as being "beaten up"). These stressors are now occurring about every other day for the past 2–3 weeks, and they may be contributing to the emergence of his depressive symptoms. He said he would like to start an antidepressant because he's worried about becoming even more depressed, even though antidepressants have not been so clearly helpful to him in the past.

I reviewed the antidepressants he's already tried, as well as the possibility of TCAs and MAOIs, though the side effects and potential lethality in overdose make these less desirable options. He's been on both Effexor and Cymbalta, so we won't try these again. He has only briefly been on Zoloft in the past (no adequate trial)—we'll try this for now; if it doesn't work, we'll try something else. The Zoloft may help with his PTSD symptoms as well. He thinks the Risperdal at 1mg is more effective than 0.5mg and is decreasing his edginess and irritability. He says that with it, he can "still have a range of feelings, including anger, but I am less chronically edgy." He is tolerating it well, with no side effects. He is also

Correspondence with the diocese of Pittsburgh . . .

tolerating Lamictal well, is now at 100mg. I said that adding an antidepressant may make it difficult to assess the effect of Lamictal versus the antidepressant, but, given that there is a delay in effectiveness and he is concerned about becoming more depressed, we could nonetheless go ahead—he understood and was agreeable to this. Seroquel at 12.5mg helps him to sleep.

[End of Medication Progress Note—Austen Riggs, Stockbridge, MA—April 26, 2010]

Session Medication Note—Austen Riggs, Stockbridge, MA—May 3, 2010

Clinical Course Since Last Note: Today, Michael reports that, since starting Zoloft, he has felt more edgy, anxious, and restless. He started to take just the Risperdal 0.5mg dose because he wasn't sure if the symptoms were a side effect of going up to 1 mg; however, he more links these symptoms to starting Zoloft. He wanted to stop the Zoloft and see if the symptoms subsided. I said that sounded like a viable option—it could be the Risperdal or the combination of Zoloft and Risperdal, but stopping one of the medications and seeing the effect, whether Zoloft or Risperdal, is a reasonable decision.

His sleep has been interrupted by feeling restless. He is having increased anxiety around memories of the car accident last month, more like he was feeling in the first few weeks afterwards (the anxiety around this had subsided somewhat). He's also been thinking about his past suicide attempts in a new light, now that he has the experience of better knowing the effect of suicide on others. However, although, on the one hand, this could be inhibitory to becoming suicidal or acting on SI, he is currently mostly feeling shame and self-criticism that he put others through this in the past. He currently denies having suicidal thoughts, although his increased anxiety has made him worry about further decompensation. Currently, he is trying to "ride the wave" and manage—he is aware of the multiple stressors he is dealing with, the car accident being a significant one but not the only one. He has noticed that he's been more withdrawn although is making an effort still to participate in the community and groups; he feels he has peers he can talk to, and he's able to turn to nursing, also.

[End of: Session Medication Note—Austen Riggs, Stockbridge, MA—May 3, 2010]

12
Lawsuit Filed

Michael with his extended family, May 2005.

Less than three months after Michael's death, my family brought suit against the diocese of Pittsburgh. Because we could not sue Dorsch and the diocese for the original crime, due to unjust statute-of-limitations laws (we would have had to file within two years of the last incident of sex abuse by Dorsch), we had to rely on the argument that the catholic church, once it started paying for Michael's mental healthcare, could not withdraw unilaterally as it wanted to do and did.

Ultimately, the courts ruled that the catholic church did not make things worse, as Michael had already tried to commit suicide in June 2008, when payments started. That, of course, is exactly wrong, as the catholic church and Dorsch started making things much worse for Michael back in 1981, but the laws prevented us from going back to the original crimes in court.

Below are the press release and fact sheet that were issued on July 29, 2010, in conjunction with the press conference we held on the same day.

For immediate release
Suit Charges Pittsburgh Diocese
Withdrawal of Assistance Leads to Suicide of Child Sexual Abuse Victim

Press Conference:
Date/Time: Thursday, July 29, 2010, 10:30 AM
Location: SPK—The Law Firm of Swensen Perer & Kontos, 2501 One Oxford Centre, Pittsburgh, Pennsylvania, 15219.
Who: Alan H. Perer, attorney for the Unglo family; Samuel J. Unglo, brother of the deceased. Also in attendance Renee Unglo (mother), Anna Unglo Dzikowski (sister), Paul M. Unglo II (brother), and Frances M. Samber (sister).

Pittsburgh, Pennsylvania—(July 29, 2010)—A lawsuit was filed Thursday morning charging that the Catholic Diocese of Pittsburgh had withdrawn

Lawsuit Filed

financial help from a sexual-abuse victim who soon after would commit suicide. The suit was filed on behalf of the man's family by Alan H. Perer, a senior attorney at SPK, the Law Firm of Swensen, Perer & Kontos. (http://spkpowerlaw.com/bios.asp#1).

Michael R. Unglo ended his own life on May 4, 2010. He was 39 years old. A doctor had warned that he was extremely unstable and needed to continue with his in-patient care. He had attempted suicide twice before.

But the care would not come. The Diocese of Pittsburgh had notified Michael's family that it would no longer be providing money for his treatment, just a few months before his death.

The reason the Diocese was paying for Michael Unglo's care was another case of sexual abuse by a clergyman. As a child, he had been sexually abused by a priest who would later be convicted of child sex abuse and serve jail time for abusing a different youth. When Bishop Zubik, head of the Pittsburgh Diocese, heard Michael's story, he had promised to do "whatever it takes to right the wrong." This was back at the end of 2008.

More than a year later, the Diocese decided it no longer would provide money for Michael's care. Alan H. Perer, one of the attorneys representing Unglo's family, described Michael as a typical victim of childhood sexual abuse. The consequences emerged to interrupt what looked like a successful, productive life.

"Michael Unglo was an honor student at the University of Pennsylvania," said Perer. "He got a job in the ad business in New York City and was quickly promoted to more and more important positions. But then things fell apart. The mental-health professionals who treated him connected his problem directly to the sexual-abuse trauma he suffered as a child.

"Even before Michael was getting treatment, he had already tried to commit suicide. It was obvious he was in trouble. It was obvious he needed help. This was not the point at which the Diocese should have decided to cut him off. Michael could have come through this and resumed a very productive life. Instead, it all fell apart, and he ended up the ultimate victim of sexual abuse."

Perer also pointed out "the irony that the priest who abused Michael Unglo is still being supported by the Diocese. After being convicted and serving jail time, the man who abused Michael in church, in the sacristy, in the confessional, on the Braille Trail in North Park, is still getting a monthly stipend and being supported by parishioners' money.

"Michael was cut off and left to sink or swim," said Perer. "But his abuser is still being taken care of."

Fact Sheet

As provided at the press conference:

    1. A complaint was filed in the Court of Common Pleas of Allegheny County, Pennsylvania, on July 28, 2010. The complaint was filed by Alan H. Perer, attorney at SPK—the Law Firm of Swensen Perer & Kontos, who represents the plaintiffs.

    2. The case is titled: SAMUEL J. UNGLO, as Administrator of the Estate of MICHAEL R. UNGLO, deceased, versus BISHOP DAVID A. ZUBIK and THE ROMAN CATHOLIC DIOCESE OF PITTSBURGH.

    3. Samuel J. Unglo is the brother of Michael R. Unglo, deceased, who at age 39, was being treated for complex post-traumatic stress disorder (PTSD) at Austen Riggs Center in Stockbridge, Massachusetts, where he committed suicide on May 4, 2010.

    4. As a child, Michael R. Unglo grew up in Etna, Pennsylvania, and attended All Saints Church. Beginning at age 10, in 1981 through

Lawsuit Filed

1985, Michael was the victim of extreme sexual abuse, committed by Richard Dorsch, then a priest at the All Saints Church.

5. Michael later attended North Catholic High School and graduated from the University of Pennsylvania with honors. He would go on to work in advertising in New York City, where he was successful professionally.

6. In 1994, Dorsch had been arrested and, in 1995, ultimately convicted of molesting a different child. He was jailed for a short period of time. Our best information is that the Diocese continues to support Dorsch with a monthly stipend.

7. On June 20, 2008, Michael attempted to take his own life. The mental-health professionals who treated him attributed his actions in significant part to the sexual abuse he suffered at the hands of Dorsch.

8. On and about July 29, 2008, the Diocese of Pittsburgh undertook to provide services to Michael Unglo that were necessary for his protection. Initially, the Diocese forwarded payment for counseling and treatment. On December 6, 2008, defendant Bishop Zubik met with the plaintiff Samuel Unglo and his brother Paul Unglo II and made a commitment to "do whatever it takes to right the wrong that was done to Michael R. Unglo by one of the church's own."

9. The Diocese subsequently provided for treatment at St. Vincent's Hospital in New York City, Mt. Sinai Hospital, and later outpatient treatment. Later, in June 2009, Michael attempted suicide for a second time in New York City. The Diocese at that time continued to provide payment for necessary services and treatment at Bellevue Hospital, at Sheppard Pratt, a residential retreat program in Baltimore, Maryland, and at Austen Riggs in Stockbridge, Massachusetts.

10. Beginning in early 2010, the Diocese indicated it would not financially support any further services or treatment, and it would issue only one final payment regardless of Michael's need for further treatment. On March 17, 2010, the Diocese forwarded a Full and Final Release for $75,000 to Michael Unglo and indicated that, whether or not the

release was signed, no further services or treatment would be provided for by the Diocese.

11. On April 5, 2010, a psychotherapist, Lee Damsky, Ph.D., at Austen Riggs Center, advised the Diocese that Michael needed continued treatment because of his "emotional dysregulation and suicidal behavior associated with his diagnoses of post-traumatic stress disorder . . . related to a history of childhood sexual abuse."

Legal Basis for the Suit

The facts of the case present a unique legal question. Could the Diocese undertake to provide necessary help to Michael Unglo and then simply stop providing help when they knew or should have known that doing so would put his life at risk?

They also had good reason to know that Michael was relying on their support and that cutting him off would cause him extreme emotional distress.

Our position is that the Diocese admitted responsibility for Michael's condition early on and acknowledged his need for serious treatment. The sudden denial of support, while Michael was still under care and clearly in need of it, could only have dire consequences. That decision by the Diocese was therefore reckless and negligent, and the consequences should have been obvious.

Compounding these actions, the Diocese can still fund resources to support Michael's abuser with monthly stipends for living expenses and perhaps even psychological counseling.

The Larger Consequences of the Diocese's Actions

Parishioners and contributors to the Diocese should know that the Diocese made the decision in this case to support the abuser but failed in its support of the victim. How often does this happen?

Announcement of the Michael R. Unglo Just Be Foundation, Inc.

In memory of Michael Unglo and so that his tragedy will not be forgotten, The Michael R. Unglo Just Be Foundation, Inc., a nonprofit charitable organization, was founded on June 16, 2010. Its purpose is to find and support other child sex abuse victims.

Part Four

More on Michael and Me

13

No Turning Back

On December 18, 2009, less than five months before Michael's third and final suicide attempt, he received the following offer of employment. He ultimately decided that he could not return to the life he knew. The pain and suffering he withstood had become so intertwined with the good he had done in his life that he could not bear the thought of returning to any piece of his life as he had previously known it.

Michael showed me the offer for employment in person when he visited us in Atlanta for Christmas that December. It is an offer that he and I, as most others, would normally jump on. However, I remember looking into his eyes and seeing that he just did not want to accept it. I told him that he did not have to take it and that we would figure it out. He did not need to put himself in a situation to work when he was still going through so much pain.

As it would turn out, that December would be the last time I would ever see Michael in person. I remember taking him to the airport. He was flying from Atlanta to Pittsburgh on December 30, 2009, to spend New Year's with the rest of our family. I dropped him off at the airport. I gave him a big hug and got a huge pit in my stomach. As we drove away from the airport, my five-year-old son, Luke, asked, "When will we see Uncle Michael again?" He started to cry. I was holding back tears myself. I told Luke that we would probably see him at Easter, but my gut told me that things might play out otherwise.

TO: Michael Unglo
CC: Florence Levitt; Bruce Rooke
FROM: Mike Muzi, Director of Staffing
DATE: December 18, 2009

We are all impressed with your credentials and are excited about the expertise and enthusiasm we believe you could bring to our organization. The following confirms the specifics of an employment offer we are pleased to extend to you:

Your title will be Group Copy Supervisor for GSW Worldwide, a member of the inVentiv Communications Inc. family of companies.

Your start date will be January 11, 2010, and you will report to Florence Levitt. Please arrive at 9:00 AM and report to the receptionist desk. Please refer to the list of acceptable employment-verification forms, and be sure to bring the appropriate document(s) with you to Orientation.

Your bi-weekly salary will be $5,384.62, which is $140,000.00 on an annual basis.

You will be eligible to participate in the company's bonus program beginning January 1, 2010. Payment of any bonus will be based on achievement against Company and individual objectives, and will be awarded in the first quarter of 2011. You must be employed by inVentiv at the time of payment to receive any bonus.

As an employee of inVentiv, you will be eligible for the following benefits:

Group health, vision, and dental insurance coverages are available. A summary of benefits is attached. You will be eligible to enroll the first day of the month coincident with or following your date of hire. You will have 30 days from your eligibility date to elect our benefits, or you will forfeit your opportunity to select coverage until the next annual open-enrollment period.

Basic life, accidental death and dismemberment, short-term disability, and long-term disability insurance coverages are company-paid benefits effective on your date of hire.

You will be eligible for 80 hours (10 days) of vacation during the first 12 months of your employment.

You will be eligible to participate in inVentiv's 401(k) plan following thirty days of employment. The company matches up to 30% of the first 6% of an employee's contributions in the first year of employment. The matching percentage is increased to 40% in the second year and 50% in the third year and beyond. Rollover money from a previous employer is accepted into the Plan immediately.

You will be required to sign a Code of Ethics Agreement. This agreement includes language which essentially disallows you from pursuing existing inVentiv Communications, Inc. clientele or active client prospects for two years following the termination of your employment with inVentiv. It also prohibits the solicitation of inVentiv employees for other employment for the same time frame.

In order to comply with the Immigration Reform and Control Act of 1986, it will be necessary for you to provide documentation verifying your citizenship for employment eligibility. You confirm that you are not subject to any contractual or other commitments, including any non-compete or severance agreement, that would restrict or conflict with your employment with inVentiv. You also understand and agree that you will be an at-will employee with inVentiv.

The Murder of Innocence

Michael, I hope that you find the terms of our offer acceptable and look forward to your affirmative response by December 22, 2009. Please indicate your acceptance of this offer by dating, signing, and returning the duplicate copy to my attention.

Accepted by: _____

Date: _____

14

Changing Your Paradigm about Loved Ones

If I have seen further it is by standing on the shoulders of Giants.
— Isaac Newton

While I cared very much about Michael and fought for him while he was going through everything the past couple years of his life, I never fully transitioned to accepting him as a victim while he was alive. What I mean by that is that there was also a part of me that wanted him to get over it and to move on. I wanted him to return to the very strong person he was for me and who helped me to succeed so much in my own life.

Michael inspired me to succeed academically and pushed me to chart new courses that I would not have otherwise decided to make had he not been in my life. I completed a summer session at Phillips Academy in Andover, Massachusetts, because of his doing. I attended Cornell University, following Michael's footsteps of going to college, something my mom and dad and three other, older siblings, never had the chance to do. I would later get a master's degree in business, also with his inspiration. He was my lighthouse growing up after losing our dad so young. It feels funny saying that, as he was only four years older, and, looking back on it, he had his own heavy and dark burden to carry himself.

In Michael's final days, he was reduced to nothing. He had to contemplate the prospect of a legal guardianship, as his following email demonstrates. Additionally, he was made to file for Social Security disability coverage, as he was paralyzed by the thought of having to work and could no longer function in the working world—and this was a man who was once thriving on Madison Avenue.

TO: Unglo, Samuel J
FROM: Michael Unglo
SENT: Saturday, April 10, 2010, 10:26 AM
SUBJECT: Planning issues

Hi, Sam—thinking of you and thinking very hard here about plans.

I'm looking into all possibilities for me to stay healthy long past my stay here. A fact I need to keep in mind is how very persistent my illness has been and continues to be. Where I'm headed with this, Sam, and this is difficult to write, is recognizing me as an adult with legal-guardianship needs.

Writing this email is difficult because it means, for me, that I have a critically impaired decision-making process. Your advocacy on my behalf, and that of healthcare pros the past several months, is a sure sign to me of this, and, at the same time, I do believe that, with the help of others, I will be able to keep up the fight against my mental illness.

Where I would like to be is with family as my legal guardian, if that is what needs to be done for me to re-emerge and participate in life beyond my stay here. I have been online this morning reading

Changing Your Paradigm about Loved Ones

about guardianship matters. I don't want to end up living precariously in a social-services setting, like what happened for me last year at Bellevue.

Tomorrow I join Aunt Dolly in being 39!

Love,
Michael

Michael knew he was slipping, but I never wanted to fully accept it. I completed his disability paperwork, but there was a part of me that was actually mad at him before he died that he was allowing this all to happen. I would come to understand only after his death—given the way in which he died—that he did not allow it to happen. The pain and burden were too much. Michael was ultimately killed by the scars of abuse, both by Dorsch and the larger wrongdoing of church leaders, not by his own doing.

Another aspect on which I have reflected is the memory of fearing he would commit suicide in our house. My wife and I contemplated having Michael live with us. There were convenient excuses: We did not necessarily have enough room, we had two young children, who gave us plenty enough to handle, etc. However, at the back of my mind was: What if he commits suicide in our house and one of our children finds him? As a parent, I found myself protecting my own children from that potentially traumatic event.

So, while we found Michael the best of mental-healthcare providers and facilities at Sheppard Pratt and Austen Riggs, what I would recommend to others with loved ones battling scars similar to Michael's or other mental-health challenges, is to keep them close in proximity so that their broader support structures are in place. Michael needed the physical presence of loved ones. He did not get that being in cities hundreds of miles from immediate family, even though he was in some of the best facilities.

15

Homelessness

*You can never go home again, but the truth is
you can never leave home, so it's all right.*
— *Maya Angelou*

One aspect of the situation in which Michael found himself that people need to understand is homelessness. Michael's sense of home was destroyed. The very church, All Saints Church, in which he was abused, sits less than a mile from my mother's home in Pittsburgh, and you pretty much have to pass by All Saints on the way to her house. That bothered Michael tremendously.

Beyond the physical dynamics of where my mom's house and All Saints Church sit in Etna, a borough of Pittsburgh, Pennsylvania, there are the emotional dynamics of having a sense of home destroyed. Michael's sense of home was shattered upon the start of his abuse. While he would ultimately have his own apartments in Philadelphia and New York, where he worked after college, he never had the sense of trust that comes with having a home.

A person who was supposed to be a loving presence for him—the very person who gave Michael his first holy communion—violated him. Father Dorsch, given his very position, was supposed to be a protector and caregiver for Michael. Yet, he was entirely the opposite. That ultimate betrayal is what undermined Michael's life after his abuse ensued. That is what so many people do not get when they tell me that abuse occurs everywhere and to go back to the catholic church. The good outweighs the bad, I am told. *Really?* I don't think so. Too many have been hurt by the catholic church and its ugly ways. They do not have policies that act for the Common Good. They act for their own good, and in so doing, cause torment for otherwise good people.

Until the catholic church acts rightly—as judged by the victims of child sex abuse, not by the supposedly infallible church leaders themselves—they will continue to cause countless others to feel homeless with respect to finding a place of peace and justice.

Michael was saddened by not having children directly—more fallout from a sense of homelessness. It was a result of his child sex abuse. However, Michael did end up having many children: the many people and loved ones he forever impacted positively.

Shortly before Michael died, my five-year-old son, Luke, unprompted and unaware of Michael's sadness at not having children directly, asked, "Who are Michael's children?" Of course, Luke does not ask many questions to which he does not already have an answer in mind. Before my wife and I could respond, he shortly followed, "We are Michael's children," referring to himself and his sister, Caitlin.

Through Michael's boundless impact on me and through Michael's great love of them while he was here, they know Michael's spirit and greatness. That said, I often grieve that he is not here to see them grow and to share in their milestones.

Michael also lost the sense of comfort that church is supposed to bring for regular churchgoers. After all, that is a main reason that they go to church—it brings them comfort. Even though Michael's innocence

Homelessness

was violated by a catholic priest, he still believed in God and tried to find comfort in the church. However, the scars were too deep, and Michael really was not able to go home to the catholic church again without negative consequences. Consider the following excerpts from his session at Austen Riggs Center (ARC) on March 11, 2010, less than two months before he died:

Session Medication Note—Austen Riggs, Stockbridge, MA—March 11, 2010

Clinical Course Since Last Note: Today's session focused on Mr. Unglo's recent experience while away at a catholic retreat. He said that one evening he was in a church chanting and praying with others and suddenly experienced a panic attack, with physical symptoms of shaking, increased heart rate, sweating, intense fear, narrowed perceptual field, and some dissociation. He felt stuck, both wanting to leave and yet not being able to. He had the thought, "Oh, no—not again," and his mind associated to his June 2009 experience that led to his hospitalization. He was able to ground himself, and the intensity of the experience dissipated after about 15 minutes. He did not spiral into a complete flashback, lose touch with where he was, or have any suicidal thoughts. The next morning, he decided to return to ARC, earlier than expected. He has since participated in a drumming workshop that had some similar contextual elements to the environment in which he had a panic attack, but he did not have one there (it was at Austen Riggs Center, with no religious references). He says that having ARC as a reference point in his mind to come back to was helpful and reassuring to him. From this experience, he realizes with greater clarity some of his vulnerabilities and how important it will be to establish a sense of community when he moves to Pittsburgh. We talked about the symptoms of panic attacks and how the environment he was in might have reminded him of his sexual abuse, even if he didn't think of it explicitly. He has not had any similar experiences since then. He is feeling anxious about leaving ARC.

Assessment (Include evaluation of effectiveness): Mr. Unglo experienced a panic attack in the context of praying and chanting at a catholic retreat center. He was able to ground himself, and the panic attack resolved in about 15 minutes. However, he decided to leave the retreat early and return to ARC. I went over the symptoms of panic attack and possible responses, and I will send him a handout about how to manage them. He has not experienced any subsequent panic attacks or emergence of PTSD symptoms. He is anxious about discharge, which is in two weeks. We discussed his discharge plans. His therapist is trying to find a psychiatrist who could offer both therapy and medication management, and I explained the rationale behind this. We will plan to meet next week.

Current risk for decompensation and/or suicidal behavior remains low at this time: He was able to work through the panic attack without further emergence of PTSD symptoms, and he did not lose touch with reality at the time. However, this panic attack does point to his vulnerabilities in regard to being in certain environments. In addition, he feels safe at ARC and recognizes he will not immediately have such a place to go to when he discharges (i.e., it will take time to build up a support system there). He plans to live with his mother initially when he gets back and is aware of the potential to isolate, which he says he has already discussed with his brother.

Homelessness

[End of: Session Medication Note—Austen Riggs, Stockbridge, MA—March 11, 2010]

This became a very rough set of circumstances. The diocese of Pittsburgh would subsequently push to cut off all ties and responsibility with a Full and Final Release in the following few weeks. Michael's only real option for free housing in Pittsburgh was at my mom's house, site of his own abuse at her hands and Dorsch's, and less than a mile up the road from All Saints Church, where Dorsch used an institution and religious setting to prey on my brother.

16

Michael's Shame and Fallout from Being Sexually Abused Ages 10-14 by a Priest

Given the nature of Michael's death and where it took place—in a full-time mental-healthcare facility—I had to ascertain his medical records, which allowed for insight that otherwise would not have been shared. The following is from Michael's medical records:

Michael reported that he was sexually abused by a priest when he was 10 through 14 years of age. He said that he had never been threatened with physical harm by the priest during that period of time, although, "With him, I think he knew how much I hated what he was doing. He would take on the role of comforting me." When asked what this was like for him, he said, "It felt okay, like it was special, like he is right, (then) it defaulted to me being his plaything." Michael reported that he was not currently experiencing flashbacks, which has been a problem for him in the past, saying, "No, I'm not. I'm really happy to say. Like in the first suicide attempt, it was in the flashback." He said at the time,

"I couldn't believe he was still haunting me. I was still stuck on that bench in the park where he did what he did."

It's not okay to be gay . . .

Growing up catholic, you are taught that it is wrong to be gay and to have those thoughts. Recently, the catholic church has progressed to thinking that it is okay to be gay as long as you do not act on those thoughts. So, it is still wrong to express who you truly are. It is not okay to be gay.

Michael was gay.

As time went on and Michael struggled with chronic PTSD, he wondered if his sexuality was influenced by his abuse. Genetically, there is a history of being gay in our family. Our uncle, our dad's brother, was gay. The family used to always want to hide that—it was not something to be proud of or to talk about openly. So, maybe Michael was gay regardless of whether the abuse had taken place. However, he struggled with the impact his abuse had on his sexuality and how he otherwise might have developed.

The triggering event on the night of Michael's first suicide attempt was a fight that he had with a boyfriend of his at the time. Michael's boyfriend informed him that evening that he had decided that he was going to become a priest. His boyfriend was going to take the path of "stopping" to be gay and to become a priest. Michael saw this as yet again being hurt by a priest. Someone he loved at the time was now turning away from him; that someone was going to be denying his own sexuality, and that someone was going to be turning back to the very institution that had hurt Michael to begin with. It was too much for Michael to handle. Michael overdosed on Ambien and tried to cut his neck. Fortunately, Michael pulled through, and it was considered "a passive suicide attempt." This is when the family truly would realize how much pain Michael was in.

Throughout all our dealings with the diocese of Pittsburgh, they would periodically ask: Why was your brother able to function "properly" before all this? What triggered this? We never told them about

Michael's Shame and Fallout from Being Sexually Abused . . .

the argument with his boyfriend's wanting to become a priest. We feared that they would be judgmental and not help him. Because of the environment of the catholic church around being gay, we did not feel comfortable telling them the truth.

Even as I decided to break the silence on many levels with this book, my brother's sexuality is one of the last things that I struggled with sharing. Should I still protect Michael? The reality is that, by not breaking the silence and telling the full truth, I would not be honoring Michael's legacy and helping others' lives to be improved by Michael's story. Yes, my brother was gay, and I was proud of that and still am.

Michael did not function "properly" before all this

The short answer to the diocese's assumption that Michael "functioned properly" until June 2008 also missed the mark. Consider the following excerpts from Michael's clinical assessments by mental-health professionals, as he was in full-time mental-healthcare facilities in 2009 and into 2010:

Consultation Note—Clinical Assessment—Austen Riggs, Stockbridge, MA—October 15, 2009

> 1. Identification of the Patient: Michael is a 38-year-old, single, gay freelance writer who had been living alone in a New York City apartment prior to recent, extended hospitalizations at Bellevue and Sheppard Pratt. He has struggled over many years with depression, anxiety, and PTSD symptoms in the context of early and extended sexual abuse by a priest. Michael was referred by his case manager at Sheppard Pratt, Kelly Shannon, and came for today's consultation accompanied by his mother, Renee, and brother, Paul.
>
> 2. Chief Complaint: "I still need to get through my chronic PTSD, and I don't want to attempt suicide a third time."

3. Presenting Problem: Michael reports that he was a lonely and isolated child who felt neglected in his large family. His father died when he was nine, and by the time he was ten, Michael was sexually abused by a priest who was a close friend of the family. This was recurrent and continued until Michael was 14, when the priest was reassigned to another parish. Michael managed this by concentrating on his schoolwork, although his self-esteem was poor, and he was socially awkward. In spite of his poor self-esteem, feelings of alienation, and rare flashbacks connected with the abuse, Michael was doing fairly well by college, and his social difficulties were dramatically decreased. After college, however, Michael's flashbacks, depression, and anxiety gradually increased, and he began treatment with antidepressants. He stopped his Effexor in 2008, in the face of worries that it was making his flashbacks more frequent, and his depression deepened. After a particularly disturbing flashback in the context of a difficult relationship, Michael decided to end his life, impulsively taking 25 Ambien along with alcohol and cutting his throat, repeatedly nicking one of his carotid arteries and losing a great deal of blood. Following a week-long psychiatric hospitalization, Michael returned to outpatient treatment, which was somewhat helpful. After this hospitalization, Michael learned that the Diocese of Pittsburgh had been legally remanded to pay for the treatment of victims of abuse by priests (although he could not press criminal charges because of a statute of limitations) and that they had been financing Michael's treatment ever since.

Michael lost a job in fall of 2008, flashbacks continued, and his depression and anxiety once again deepened. In 4/09, after an altercation with his lover, Michael became extremely upset and called his sister-in-law. She told him that he wasn't making sense and called 911. Michael was taken to Bellevue

Michael's Shame and Fallout from Being Sexually Abused . . .

but was released after a day or two in their ER. Following his acceptance to their MFA program, Michael attended a weeklong summer writing workshop at Sarah Lawrence and returned to New York on 6/26/09 (days after the anniversary of his previous suicide attempt) increasingly upset and wounded by the critique of his writing, "and I fell apart." He returned to his apartment to find the toilet clogged and overflowing with feces, and he became paranoid that someone had broken in while he was away. (Michael admitted to worrying that the family of his ex-lover was after him, to writing strange things on photographs and mailing them to his own family members, and to referring to himself as "Michelle" recently.) Michael then left his apartment wearing an odd assortment of clothing and paced the city for a while, deciding "I'm done." He returned to his 4th-floor apartment with the conviction that he could not kill himself before he threw his possessions out of the window, throwing diplomas and other things into the back courtyard so that no one would be hurt. Then, reportedly feeling that he didn't want to die "alone," he climbed out his front window, leaving his legs locked inside of it but the rest of his body dangling outside, holding some cable wires. He also apparently heard a voice telling him NOT to kill himself. Michael was then involuntarily admitted to Bellevue, where he stayed for nearly three weeks and reportedly showed psychotic behavior. He was then transferred to Sheppard Pratt, where he remained for more than two months, the first week on a locked unit. Michael experienced Sheppard Pratt as "a safe refuge," and further treatment at Riggs was recommended.

Michael reports low-grade depressive symptoms since childhood and about a dozen more-serious periods of depression beginning in college. These involve a depressed mood, initial insomnia, low energy, decreased appetite (with up to a 15-pound weight loss), decreased libido, anhedonia, social isolation, feelings of hopelessness and guilt, and suicidal thoughts. Michael reports that the latter have not been frequent or sustained, occurring primarily around the times of his hospitalizations.

Michael seems to have had periods (lasting up to 2 and ½ days) of hypomanic symptoms, with sleeplessness, pressured speech and racing thoughts, euphoria, impulsivity, and irritability.

PTSD symptoms have included intermittent flashbacks (the last about two weeks ago), detachment and numbing in relationships, startling, and re-experiencing trauma. He denies nightmares connected with the abuse. (Michael has also had panic attacks, although further history will have to be gathered about their nature and whether they occur independently of the PTSD.)

Other traumatic experiences include an incident in 1998 when Michael and another man leaving a gay bar were pelted with eggs and then physically assaulted by other men, who threw some punches and then sped off in their car, and a date-rape/sexual assault in 2002. There is no history of an eating disorder. Michael describes romantic relationships in ways that suggest they are somewhat disconnected and turbulent.

4. Pertinent Past Psychiatric History: Michael did not have any treatment before he began seeing a therapist after a flashback-triggered depression in 1997. His treatment over time seems to have been intermittent and disjointed. He saw his initial therapist for about four months and found the treatment (which involved meditation) helpful, and it was around this time that Michael first told his friends that he had been abused. He re-entered treatment in 2000 in New York City in the context of feeling angry that he was

Michael's Shame and Fallout from Being Sexually Abused . . .

haunted by flashbacks. He saw a psychiatrist for medications after the traumatic terrorism in 2001 but had only brief meetings and did not speak about the abuse. Michael seems to have later resumed psycho-pharmaceutical treatment and took Effexor throughout 2007 and the first part of 2008. He was first hospitalized in 2008 (medical treatment at St. Vincent's, followed by about a week at Mt. Sinai) after he made an impulsive but life-threatening suicide attempt in the context of having an extremely disturbing flashback. Afterward, he began seeing a trauma therapist, and this treatment helped somewhat. Michael's more recent hospitalizations are described above.

5. Pertinent Family/Social History: Michael's paternal grandmother had an unknown psychiatric problem for which she was hospitalized/institutionalized for several months in the 1950s. This resolved, and she afterward reportedly functioned well. There is no other known family history of significant mental illness, substance abuse, or completed suicide.

As above, Michael grew up shy, lonely, and isolated, the fourth child in a sibship of five. He felt overlooked and angry in his family, engaging in solitary activities and doing well academically. His father died unexpectedly when Michael was nine, and he remembers being given the news by his mother and the local parish priest, who had then become part of the household, frequently attending meals and holidays. Michael remembers crying continually for about a week following his father's death. Michael also recalls going to the parish house (which he experienced as "a safe haven") after mass and sitting with this priest on a sofa watching television. The man eventually had Michael perform oral sex on him and later took Michael on day trips, sexually abusing him in other locations, often outdoors, such as parks. This began when Michael was 10 and stopped when he was 14, after the priest was assigned to another parish. Michael was very angry when his mother threw the priest a going-away party at their house. Michael did not speak with his family about the abuse until 1995. His mother could not believe that this had happened because they had known the priest well, and he had been close with the family.

Michael was less isolated in high school, where he was involved in a number of extracurricular activities, but his self-esteem was low, and he was socially awkward. He graduated in 1989 and went to the University of Pennsylvania. Here Michael had difficulty in finding a good balance between partying and his academics but did much better socially. He had had a variety of jobs since, living in Philadelphia, Boston, and New York, where he lost his most recent job, doing pharmaceutical copywriting, in the fall of 2008, and afterward worked as a freelance writer, last working earlier this year. Michael has been accepted by the MFA writing program at Sarah Lawrence College and has been given a deferral through the fall of 2010. Michael describes relationships with men in a way which suggested that they have been somewhat superficial and unstable.

6. Substance Abuse History: Michael does not smoke cigarettes. He used marijuana infrequently (about twice per year) during college, never more often than this, and he reports last smoking pot in 1/06. Michael first drank alcohol at age 17, and, although he was never a daily drinker, he began significant binge-drinking during college, becoming physically sick a number of times but never having a blackout or withdrawal symptoms. This pattern continued until about 2004. He was sexually assaulted once while drunk; he went home with a man from a bar and woke in the middle of the night when the man was attempting to have anal sex. Over

Michael's Shame and Fallout from Being Sexually Abused . . .

more recent years, Michael has drunk significantly less but has partied intermittently, often drinking a lot. He reports that he last drank in 6/09. He used cocaine three times in 2003, but not since. Michael has tried ecstasy, last using this drug in 1999. He has not used other drugs and denies any abuse of prescription medications (other than when he took an overdose of Ambien).

7. Suicide History (include current suicidal ideation or intent): Michael first had a brief flash of suicidal ideation in 1998, when he thought about driving off a bridge. He had more serious suicidal ideation in 2008, when he impulsively made a potentially lethal suicide attempt (on 6/20/08) without planning ahead of time or writing a suicide note. This was in the context of ambivalence about living in New York and a relationship that had become contentious. Michael took an overdose of 25 tablets of Ambien combined with alcohol, and he cut his neck. He was discovered by a friend and taken to St. Vincent's ER. Michael reportedly nicked one of his carotid arteries, losing a tremendous amount of blood and requiring a transfusion. The context and details of Michael's more recent suicide attempt are provided above.

Michael denied having any suicidal ideation over recent weeks, including on the day of admission.

[End of: Consultation Note—Clinical Assessment—Austen Riggs, Stockbridge, MA—October 15, 2009]

Further, Michael's initial psychopharmacology assessment at Austen Riggs shows that he was not "functioning properly" until June 20, 2008, the date of his first suicide attempt.

Initial Psychopharmacology Contact Note—Austen Riggs, Stockbridge, MA—October 15, 2009

Medication history (from the patient):

1997—Reached out to a mental-health professional for the first time and saw a psychologist who didn't recommend meds at the time but did CBT (cognitive behavioral therapy) and reframing and meditation therapy, which stopped his flashbacks and helped him for three years.

November 2000—Flashbacks started again; was using drugs and alcohol heavily; family was concerned.

September 11, 2001—Sadness in friends over the events prompted Michael to discuss his depression (not his abuse history), and they convinced him to get help.

2002—Started on Zoloft, which was his first psychiatric medicine. He took it for four months and said it didn't help.

2003–2004—Took Celexa; initially it helped but then stopped working.

2006—Took Cymbalta, may have helped, but he gained weight, so he stopped it.

Summer 2007—Effexor worked but then stopped working prior to his suicide attempt.

June 20, 2008—OD on Ambien.

2008 after first suicide attempt—Started Prozac, and it was increased to 40mg but didn't help.

July 2009—Started Risperdal due to psychosis but had stopped it, along with Prozac, by September 1, due to resolution of psychosis and depression and his desire to "not be in a fog."

Michael's Shame and Fallout from Being Sexually Abused . . .

[End of: Initial Psychopharmacology Contact Note—Austen Riggs, Stockbridge, MA—October 15, 2009]

Another excerpt from Michael's medical records provides further context to his state of mind and the fallout from having to live with and process the sickening sex abuse that he suffered at the hands of Dorsch from age ten to age fourteen.

Comprehensive Psychopharmacology Evaluation Note—Austen Riggs, Stockbridge, MA—November 27, 2009

Past Psychiatric History (hospitalizations, substance abuse history, suicide, assault and trauma history); Prior Inpatient Hospitalizations:

June 2008: St. Vincent's for three days after impulsive suicide attempt in the context of drinking alcohol and multiple stressors: took 25 Ambien pills and Tylenol PM, and cut his neck. He was found in the morning in the bathtub by his ex-partner, was taken to the ER by EMTs, admitted to the ICU, intubated.

Transferred to Mt. Sinai after being medically stabilized at St. Vincent's. Hospitalized for a week. This was followed by intensive outpatient treatment, including six-week group counseling to address binge drinking.

April 2009: Brief, 48-hour stay at Bellevue for depression, high state of anxiety, not making sense that concerned his sister-in-law when he was on the phone with her (appears he had a flashback while talking to her). She called his brother, who called EMS. At Bellevue, he presented as disorganized in his thought process; he denied suicidal ideation (SI) and homicidal ideation (HI); the differential, as with Sheppard Pratt, was whether his symptoms were more reflective of a dissociative process versus psychosis. He was given Haldol 5mg and Ativan 2mg for extreme anxiety/agitation, felt much better the day after admission, and presented much more clearly. He reported not having had anything to drink in three days, although other reports state that he had been drinking. Collateral information given by his sister-in-law: she reported that her brother had been deteriorating for about a week; he evidently noticed that he was "not himself" and was disoriented. Therapist also interviewed. Acute stressors included ex-partner calling to wish him a happy birthday and Michael feeling scared of him due to a fight; the day before presentation to Bellevue, his ex-boyfriend had left messages demanding some of his possessions be returned. Also had recent birthday celebration; many friends came, but he felt dissociated during it. Later attended Easter mass, which also may have been a trigger. He had an argument with a friend and began to experience flashbacks and memories of past abuse. In therapy, had vivid episode of re-experiencing, described as a "full-blown epileptic flashback," though calmed by the end of the session. His psychiatrist, Dr. Filova, was also contacted. She had last seen him in February 2008. He had made so much progress in treatment that she was seeing him less often, although she had heard from the therapist that he had recently experienced a severe flashback during a therapy session.

June 2009: Bellevue Hospital (ER/inpatient unit): After hanging out of his window holding onto cable wires, police carried him inside, and he was taken to Bellevue. Hospitalized for three weeks.

Notes from Bellevue: Family members state patient had become more isolated and paranoid since being laid off from his job in April 2009. Patient was also briefly hospitalized at Bellevue in April (see above). After this, he became anxious

Michael's Shame and Fallout from Being Sexually Abused...

that his ex-boyfriend was stalking him. He also began to engage in risky sexual behaviors (e.g., group sex and sex with friends), which was unusual for him. In late May/early June, he was sent a box of old photographs, which he had requested his mother send in the past; she just hadn't done so until then. He became upset when he looked at them, because some dated to the time he was sexually molested by a priest, including photographs of the priest. He thought his mother was minimizing what had happened to him by sending these photos. He then became increasingly odd in his behavior, sending 2–15 family pictures to his siblings daily with commentary on the back, describing what the people in the photos "were really thinking," signing them with his pen name, Michael Onelight. He also stated a belief that his great-aunt was really his mother and that his family had kept this information from him. On the night of his second suicide attempt, he returned from a writing workshop, found his toilet clogged up with feces, and reported overhearing a group of people outside making derogatory comments about him, including accusing him of being a "fag." He said he didn't know who they were, although they called him by his name. He then proceeded to throw items from his apartment out into a vacant courtyard, including an eight-foot mirror and expensive art work (one item supposedly worth $6,000). What happened next was not clear—he took back his initial claim of having taken 30 of his Prozac 20mg tablets. He reported sitting at his window, intending to jump. He said he had the thought, "What's the point? I might as well jump." He denied feeling depressed prior to this event or having any suicidal ideation or plans. However, when his sister went to his apartment following his suicide attempt, she found the only clothing left there was a black suit and black tie, which she assumed he intended to be his funeral clothing had he died (of note, this also could be seen as the clothing of a priest). The patient did recall NYPD officers breaking into his apartment and pulling him from the window, cuffing him, and bringing him in for a psychiatric evaluation. On presentation, he did not make sense, making statements such as "no place, place no." He was "oddly related, appeared internally preoccupied, and his eyes were darting around the room." He had an empty bottle of Prozac on him and stated he had taken all the pills in his bottle. There is also mention he hadn't been taking his Prozac in the past month. In the evaluation room, he became agitated, requiring physical restraints, and received Valium 5mg. He denied recent insomnia, anhedonia, feelings of guilt, decreased energy or appetite, problems concentrating, or suicidal ideation. He was transferred to an inpatient unit at Bellevue. He initially appeared paranoid, frequently looking around the room or turning his head quickly to look outside it. He appeared very guarded and refused to answer some of the questions about recent events. He provided limited past history. His sister Anna reported that he had called her after being admitted, initially telling her how he had come to the hospital but then beginning to talk about a conspiracy and that he had "uncovered the greatest revelation and deepest secret," that he "was not really himself," and that his parents were not his actual parents. His Prozac was restarted, and he was started on Risperdal, titrated up to 2mg in the AM and 3mg in the PM. By the second week of his hospitalization, he was less guarded and less internally preoccupied, but remained off (e.g., calling his family pretending to be someone else) and continued to believe that he was not the biological child of his parents. He believed that staff had tried to poison him during his April admission. He also believed his landlord had broken into his apartment while he was away. Over the following week, he became somatically preoccupied, with complaints of heartburn/indigestion, hemorrhoids, unexplained bruising,

Michael's Shame and Fallout from Being Sexually Abused . . .

and lightheadedness. He denied auditory hallucinations (AH), visual hallucinations (VH), suicidal ideation (SI), and homicidal ideation (HI). Plans were made to transfer him to Sheppard Pratt as he was quite devaluing his treatment at Bellevue. He was transferred to Sheppard Pratt on July 16, 2009. Given his bizarre behavior at the time of presentation to Bellevue and in the months leading up to his second suicide attempt, a primary psychotic disorder was considered in the differential diagnosis Schizophreniform Disorder (D/O). His second suicide attempt appeared to be in the context of psychosis.

Sheppard Pratt: Spent almost two months there, learned coping skills, found this hospitalization helpful. Transferred from Sheppard Pratt to Austen Riggs Center. Discharge notes from Sheppard Pratt (10/14/2009): "Transferred to The Retreat after a serious suicide attempt. He was weaned off his medications at his insistence and against their advice. He was eager to reconnect with his family to increase his sense of support. Primary difficulties were thought to stem from a chronic, severe PTSD induced by the sexual abuse by the priest who was a friend of the family. He has had increased symptoms, particularly depersonalization/derealization and flashbacks in the past three years prior to admission. Incidents related to his trauma history were prominent in both suicide attempts. He made significant progress while at Sheppard Pratt. In October, he had been off his medications for six weeks and had maintained a stable mood and normal thinking process, without psychotic symptoms. By October, he no longer had any suicidal ideation. Because of his chronic PTSD and recent psychotic depression, continued treatment in a residential setting was recommended."

Medication changes: Admitted on Risperdal 5mg daily, which was tapered to 2mg daily. Mr. Unglo continued to complain of "fogginess in the head" and wanted to go off it, although this was not recommended by the psychopharmacologist, who thought he should remain on it for several more months. Mr. Unglo also insisted on stopping his Prozac. He tolerated the process of stopping his medications well and also did well off medications.

Discharge Diagnoses:

- PTSD, severe, chronic (Primary Diagnosis)
- Major Depression, recurrent (resolved)
- Psychosis Not Otherwise Specified (NOS) (resolved)
- Mixed Personality Disorder with Narcissistic and Passive Aggressive Features
- Etiology of his psychosis was unclear at time of discharge. It seemed related to his trauma symptoms but also somewhat out of proportion to them. There was considered not enough evidence to definitely give a diagnosis of a primary psychotic disorder at time of discharge.

[End of: Comprehensive Psychopharmacology Evaluation Note—Austen Riggs, Stockbridge, MA—November 27, 2009]

"Was he married?"
As I tell Michael's story to some and they find out that he was 39 when he died, a common question seems to be: "Was he married?" When I say that he was not, people seem almost relieved. Well, at least no one else was affected—his wife or any children.

What about all the other ones he left behind? What about our pain? We do not necessarily want sympathy. What we want is the proper honoring of his life and the understanding of his story.

Some have told us that Michael was gay; thus, they believe that he was sort of predisposed to the abuse anyway and might have enjoyed

Michael's Shame and Fallout from Being Sexually Abused . . .

some aspects of the sex that took place. Whether someone is gay or not, it is statutory rape for someone over the age of 18 to have sex with someone under the age of 18. At the age of 10, Michael was not in a position to determine his sexuality, and the fact that he was ultimately gay does not excuse that Dorsch sexually abused him.

Part Five

Grieving and Evolving

17

My Grieving Process

In the depth of winter, I finally learned that there was within me an invincible summer.
— Albert Camus

If you're going through hell, keep going.
— Winston Churchill

I tend to like things to happen fast. I am not the most patient person in the world. At different points since the day my brother died, I thought I was most of the way through the grieving process, but I was not. I wrote his eulogy, which I include in this chapter. It set a blueprint for me, and I wanted to move forward quickly to make a positive difference. I set up Michael's foundation all in a few months after he died. I trained hard to run a marathon in his honor and wrote a reflection on that run, also included in this chapter.

That marathon was February 2011. I thought after that I would be coming along pretty well in my grieving process, but I was not. From February 2011 through May 2014, there would be many times that I wanted to write this book, but I could not complete it. The theme and spirit of it just was not there. I was either too sad to write, wanted to avoid the pain, or was outright angry about all that had happened. I was pissed off that I had to write a book because this tragedy had happened.

In my journey since Michael's death, I knew I had to change course along the way.

I mixed things up. I had a great opportunity to switch jobs and to take a few weeks off in between jobs. I was able to do nothing for once—something I had not had time to do since my brother died. That quiet time allowed me to get comfortable with getting to a point where I realized it is simply about sharing Michael's life so that people know it all. Once that is done, I can be more at peace with where things are because I will have broken the silence more fully—no more feeling that there is something still unspoken or incomplete about his life.

Michael's Eulogy

Michael's eulogy contained four main sections: the main eulogy, a writing I wrote prior to his death that I wanted to read to him one last time, a letter a friend of Michael sent to me in the early-morning hours on the day of Michael's funeral, and a letter my sister Frances wrote to Michael. I delivered the first three sections to the congregation with the fourth, Frances's letter, read by my brother-in-law, Brian, on her behalf. Michael's friend did not necessarily intend for me to read his letter during Michael's eulogy, but I found it to be a wonderful example of the great friend many found in Michael. His friend's letter seemed to express so properly who Michael was and what we lost.

Michael Ralph Unglo (April 11, 1971, to May 4, 2010)—Eulogy

By Sam Unglo. As delivered at Christ Episcopal Church, North Hills, 5910 Babcock Boulevard, Pittsburgh, Pennsylvania, 15237, on May 11, 2010.

My dear brother, where to begin?

My Grieving Process

First, thank you. Thank you for all the time you were with us. We will miss you more than you will ever know. The overwhelming outpouring of love by those here today is representative of all the lives you impacted positively. You were a great friend and loving presence to so many.

My memories of you will always be great. Our boyhood years were entertaining and fun. You nicknamed me "Orca," as I was quite plump around the midsection. I nicknamed you "Pinocchio," because your nose was a little bigger than most. And there was the mutual term of endearment that we had, "Bubba," which you came up with upon chewing some Hubba Bubba gum.

As we grew up, it became clear to all that you were one who would never accept the status quo. You would become more than anyone's expectations, you would define your own expectations, and you would inspire others to do the same. You were the first in our immediate family to graduate from college—and not just any college. You went after the very best—you graduated from the University of Pennsylvania, one of the original four Ivy League schools, one of the world's finest. I always found it amusing that Penn was your safety school.

At Penn, you excelled in both academics and extracurricular activities. You led activist marches and became president of a fraternity. Leadership and courage were always on display as you embraced new frontiers. Truth and purity of thought were at the heart of your actions.

You inspired me to go after new frontiers, too, joining you in the college ranks and the Ivy League. Many have said that we stand on the shoulders of those who have gone before us, and I can only say the same as you positioned and inspired me to go after more and more and to dream big.

After Penn, you began an excellent career that spanned many years in medical advertising and creativity. You were accomplished in creating new campaigns and slogans for drugs targeting cardiac care, HIV treatment, and antibacterial infections. At each challenge, you stood and delivered.

You were always setting new firsts and inspired me to take up running marathons. We completed three together: the New York City Marathon in 2004, Atlanta in 2007, and the Rome, Italy, Marathon in 2008. They were all great runs, but I think you know New York was my favorite with you. It was a brilliant day, you were on your game, and I had to keep up. As always, you were running strong ahead of the pack and setting the vision. I wrote a poem commemorating that day, which I'll share with everyone a little later.

And sadly, brother, while you were achieving all of the above, you suffered far too long in silence with a burden that you started to bear at too young an age—that no one should have to bear at any age. At the time when our family trusted someone the most, that very person violated us the most. Shortly after Dad died in 1981, we now know that you went through torture the next four years, being abused and tormented by a roman catholic priest who would finally be convicted years later for his crimes against children.

Family and friends here today, what you have come to read about regarding the roman catholic church and priests abusing children is far too common and true. That is why we are not sitting in a roman catholic church today. The leaders of that church must change—plain and simple. In Michael's hour of need, the roman catholic church failed him—and us—yet again.

Many of you have probably seen the movie *The Blind Side,* which came out late in 2009. In that movie, an essay is written. One of the quotes from the essay is, "And maybe even pray that the people telling you what to do have some [honor],

My Grieving Process

too." Far too many people abuse the power of their positions. Honor is all about never losing sight of truth and beauty and protecting those precious gifts when we are entrusted with doing so. Michael did exactly that throughout his life. Michael was a victim of an extremely dishonorable man and the men in an institution who work to hide such perpetrators, and in so doing, become perpetrators themselves no less guilty; and we lament their actions.

Brother, you always went after things with passion and conviction. I want to remind everyone here today of a famous inscribed archway at Penn, which, translated into English, reads, "We will find a way, or we will make one." Additionally, the official motto of the University of Pennsylvania is, "Laws without morals are in vain." These two phrases are very appropriate to remember as I promise you, brother, that we will do everything in our power to hold the people accountable for what you had to suffer. Laws and statutes of limitations have been set up to protect the guilty, but we will find a way—or make one—to hold them accountable. Your life will be honored and your suffering remembered.

Brother, the comfort I find today is that I know you are suffering no longer. I cannot begin to imagine the daily pain and torment you went through with your burdens. The past two years were especially tough and hard on you as you dealt with violent flashbacks and complex post-traumatic stress disorder. I know that God loves you and has taken you home to be with our other loved ones.

Have fun with Dad in heaven. I am sure you are finally hearing firsthand how proud of you he is. May you finally get some rest and be at peace. I love you.

And now that poem I promised . . .

Two Brothers—New York City Marathon
November 7, 2004
By Sam Unglo

The alarm clocks ring. It's 4:30 AM. We get ready—although preparations for this race started long before today—and leave for the bus ride across the Verrazano-Narrows Bridge.

We are all runners on the bus. As we look toward the skies—radiant with the brilliance of a new dawn—we find inspiration. We think about how long we have waited for this. Can we do this for the first time? Can we run another marathon? Yes, we can.

We arrive at the start line. It's 6:45 AM. Start time is 10:10 AM. We occupy our time with staying warm and discover that plastic garbage bags can be quite insulating. We eat a light breakfast—twice—enjoy free samples of POM Wonderful pomegranate juice, make several trips to the Portajohns, sleep, and watch the sun rise farther away from the horizon and higher into the sky.

The start is almost here. We shed our plastic bags, sweatpants, and sweatshirts. We tell each other, "I love you" and know that this is a day to remember. The national anthem is sung as we move toward the start. We take heart in knowing that we have each other by our side.

The cannon blasts! The start is here. We move onto the Verrazano-Narrows Bridge and, mid-span, feel the rhythmic tension unique to a suspension bridge. The first few miles fly by as we make our way from Staten Island into Brooklyn.

The temperature, once cold, is now getting quite warm by runner, and even spectator, standards. We shed our long-sleeve Dri-FIT shirts and put the short-sleeve ones back on. Another mile goes by, and in a stunning display, we go a few

My Grieving Process

cars deep on a side street and strip down, shedding our Dri-FIT tights so that we end up with just shorts.

We hear shouts: "Go, Sam!" and "Go, Lungs!" As marathon runners do, we opted to put our names on our shirts. Michael went with "Ungs," a shortened, endearing form of our last name, although some spectators thought it read "Lungs."

The Queensboro Bridge looms in the distance as we hit miles 10 and 11. We know that it will be mile 15 before we are on the bridge. We hit the halfway mark, 13.1 miles, at 2:04:51 (Michael) and 2:04:52.

Mile 17 starts as we enter Manhattan. The wall of roars greets us as we begin our journey through Manhattan up to the Bronx and back to Manhattan to finish in Central Park.

As mile 20 nears, the legs start to feel heavier. The remaining miles are where one becomes a marathoner. We're up for the challenge.

Michael has the first-time marathon glow. Around mile 22, he knows that he will finish his first marathon—it's just a matter of time—and encourages Sam to finish strong with him.

Mile 24, and we're almost home. We're in the zone. The crowds in Central Park are incredible, and one runner is particularly vocal and animated, screaming, "Viva New Jersey! Viva New Jersey!" Sam laughs as the runner proceeds to yell this for the next two miles.

We're running down Central Park South. The finish line is less than a mile away. A few more minutes, and yes, we see the finish line.

We quickly approach—our legs feeling fresh once again—lock our hands, and raise our arms high. We just finished the New York City Marathon! The race is over, and memories for a lifetime have just begun.

The Murder of Innocence

TO: Unglo, Samuel J
FROM: Michael Evashevski
SENT: Monday, May 10, 2010 2:15 AM
SUBJECT: Michael

Hi, Sam,

I'm writing this, sadly, because I can't be there to say it in person on Monday and Tuesday. An email isn't my desired way of writing this, but I don't want it to wait, or have a letter not reach you and your family in time. How I feel about your brother and my friend, Michael, as hard as I try, can never be summarized by words or letters. As I write this, I find that it's partly just for me to render the memory of him clearly, but despite that, I hope this helps you and your family—whom I've come to know—know what Michael meant to me.

I met Michael, as you know, under unusual circumstances, the night after we had both run the New York City Marathon. It was a party that claimed to be for both of us, but later we used to joke over whose party it really was. I was graduating school and interviewing for a job in Boston while Michael lived there. His generosity was apparent; he couldn't have been happier to have me stay with him, even though we hardly knew each other at the time. Most of me felt like I'd known him forever.

Later, after I had decided to move to New York, he also had moved back to Manhattan that summer. I found him exciting, always passionate, always centered, and having a unique perspective on life and the things I was then only growing to understand. Somehow he lived life like it was made for him. We would visit museums or go on long runs, and we'd end up meeting someone new everywhere we went. Michael was magnetic like that; he had something that pulled you into him. He was fun, vibrant, and never afraid to take what we all deserve out of the world.

We shared many things in the more-than five years we knew each other, and I owe much to what he's given me: conversations that

My Grieving Process

widened my perspectives, finding my first apartment in New York and the great people I met there, my first taste of tea, trips outside of the city with my now-friend Paul, even my partner Bill. My world would be a very different place without Michael.

I can't ever remember him unhappy—at least he never showed it. Even when I'd visit him at Bellevue hospital, he would draw pictures for me, write poetry, and be 100% set on making wherever he was a better place. It made no difference where he was: people were always people at their core to Michael, and his ability to see the qualities that really mattered in others is, among many other things, something I feel fortunate to take from him.

I last spoke to Michael near his birthday. I had hoped he would take me up on my offer to come back to visit for a little while. Now I wish I would have had the perspective to visit him instead.

I wish many things, but maybe regrets are common. Maybe I could have stayed out later that night. Maybe I could have called him when I didn't. For me, I guess it's maybe difficult to look back on someone like Michael, only because I don't want to come to realize what I've lost, or what my future will be without the good he had to give. But I'll always remember him. I don't have photographs of the things and times with Michael that mean most to me, but I think that's what makes them special—it's what keeps him alive when I feel lonelier for not having him around.

Even if he didn't feel this world was made for him, I just hope he knew how much I cared about him. I just hope he knows how much I miss him.

Please share my thoughts and love with the rest of your family, and let them know what Michael meant to me.

Love, Michael Evashevski

The Murder of Innocence

Frances's Letter to Michael (fourth section of Michael's eulogy)

Michael,

I don't know where to begin. How can I or anyone put into words the beauty you brought to everyone's life? You are my brother, one of my best friends, my confidant, my inspiration, my hero.

I have so many childhood memories that make me laugh. I remember the times when we would try to scare each other when mom would send us to our rooms for not listening. We would sit at the top of the stairs because we were too afraid to go back into our rooms after all the scary stories we'd tell each other. And when we would act so silly at dinner time, trying to see who could come up with the silliest names to call each other, such as, "ketchup bottle, mustard head, and telephone pole." I know it sounds so crazy now, but we would laugh for hours. I remember playing in the yard with neighborhood friends and doing chores on Saturday mornings.

It seems we all grew up so fast. In the blink of an eye, you were off to college and moved away. But then came the visits. How I loved visiting you in Philadelphia! I'll never forget the White Dog Café and the peach cobbler. I remember loading the moving trucks and drinking espresso before bedtime. My trips to New York City were always full of adventure and always lots of fun. Broadway plays and the crazy subway stations always left us wanting more.

I'll never forget all your visits to Harrisburg, all the Chinese take-out, all the visits to Lancaster and Hershey Chocolate World—and who could forget the trips to my doctor appointments?

My Grieving Process

You have such an energy about you. Just being near you makes me and everyone else a better person. You are the best labor coach any expecting mom could ever wish for.

I am truly blessed to have a brother like you. You gave me encouragement when I was doubtful; you gave me strength when I was weak. You set such high expectations for yourself, and you met every one of them, teaching me that nothing in life is out of reach. Sometimes I don't know where you found the discipline. I'm still searching.

Some people are very lucky to go through life with little or no tragedies to interfere with who they are to become. And others carry burdens that sometimes get too heavy to bear.

You have faced so many challenges, and you battled each one with strength and dignity. I know in life we must say goodbye to our loved ones. But this goodbye is too soon. You are too beautiful to be still. I am not ready to let you go. I'm not ready to say goodbye. We have so many unfinished conversations and so many more memories that were just waiting to happen. I have no idea what I'm going to do without you. You are such a big part of my life.

I can't see you anymore, but I feel you everywhere. I will take you with me on my journey through this world. I will think of you every minute until I take my last breath. You will always be alive within my heart. You live through me now and everyone else who knew and loved you.

Because you are within us, you will still laugh and cry, sing and dance, feel the sun and wind on your face. Read bedtime stories and kiss our children goodnight. You live because we live.

Thank you for all the memories, for the happy times, the sad times, the difficult moments, and the unforgettable joys and sorrows.

You have been the best brother, son, uncle, godfather, and friend anyone could ever wish to know.

Your story and your memories will live on.

I wish you nothing but Peace on your next journey.

I love you,
Your big sister, (AKA Subba) Fran

The time after Michael's funeral was incredibly hard. Looking back on it, I was incredibly angry.

One of the hardest things I have ever had to do was to tell my son, Luke, that Uncle Michael had passed away. Luke and Michael had a very special bond. Michael treated him like a son, and I could see the joy that Luke brought to Michael. I could see in Michael his love for Luke's innocence, wanting to protect that innocence, and to have fun with him. It was as if Michael tried to relive his own innocence by relating and playing with Luke when he would visit us in Atlanta on his trips down from New York.

It was extremely painful for me to tell Luke that Michael had passed away. I could not tell him all the details, of course. He was only five years old, and I was still trying to process it all myself. My almost two-year-old daughter, Caitlin, did not even get a chance to know Michael. That was a different kind of hurt and brought on even more anger in the early weeks after Michael's death.

I turned my energy to creating Michael's foundation and training to run a marathon in his honor. I wrote the following after training

My Grieving Process

and running the Mardi Gras Marathon in New Orleans, Louisiana, on February 13, 2011:

The Wind at My Back

It's race day. It's 4:30 AM in New Orleans, Louisiana. While many are still recovering from misspent nights on Bourbon Street, there are still many others getting ready for a marathon. How will the day turn out? Always a big question for marathon runners as the 26.2 miles loom.

Today's my 26th marathon, and it never gets old. Marathons take on new and different meanings as life continues to unfold. I do my usual morning routine, fueling up on Gatorade, eating a couple Snickers Marathon bars, and then heading to the start line, 1.5 miles from the hotel. Before I head out, I take one last look in the mirror for a gut check and say, "This one's for you, Michael," as I dedicate this race to my brother, who is now watching from above.

I get to the start and in an instant know this is going to be a special day. The first full song I hear starts from the top: It's "Human" by The Killers. The lyrics include, "Are we human, or are we dancer?" While every artist has his intention for his work, the beauty of art is that it lets those observing build and come up with their own meaning. For me, this song is a reminder to consider whether we are merely human or if we can rise above the basics of being human and be more—much more—just as Michael demonstrated throughout his life.

The race begins. It's a perfect day: about 40 degrees Fahrenheit to start, not getting above 50 before expected finish time, and the course is flat and fast, just asking for a personal record (PR). As the previous 25 marathons have taught, a PR happens from a race run smartly, containing the initial rush of adrenaline and unleashing it smoothly throughout the race with the ultimate goal of finishing faster than when starting. The first seven miles go by easily as I run sub-8:00 miles. Reality check: Am I starting off too fast? I try to hold back a little to make sure I'm not overexerting, but 14 miles in, I'm still yielding sub-8:00s. Miles 15–20 see me slow a little, as the third quarter of a marathon usually proves to be a little tougher all around, but as I start into the 20s, there is still plenty of gas left in the tank.

This is one of the greatest feelings in the world: running a marathon smartly and knowing that, with six miles to go, you can attack the course, and that's exactly what I do. As I run between miles 21 and 22, I run alongside beautiful Lake Ponchartrain and feel an extra presence: those watching from above, whom I miss dearly down here, namely my Dad and Michael, are inspiring a strong finish. The wind is at my back. They propel me forward, not just now but long after today's race is over. Their hopes and dreams for me demand ongoing discipline to give life the best I have and to chart new frontiers for myself and my family. Leaving a great legacy requires elevating the lives of loved ones and inspiring them to achieve their own sense of greatness.

The rest of the race is history. It's an awesome series of moments. I run faster than I have any six-mile portion of the race. The strides are effortless. This is my time to shine. Everything is clicking and working on all cylinders. These are the moments from which I will draw upon in the future to know I can do anything and that there are still great times ahead. And there is always the hope that there will be more and more days when the wind is at my back and when effort and hard work lead to those memorable days where it all comes together, and all is possible. Perhaps, one of today's lessons from above is that, when you train hard, work hard, and focus on the fundamentals, the bigger picture has a way of taking care of itself, and you surprise even yourself.

The finish line is ahead—time for one last surge. As I near it, my right hand donning one of the final gifts my brother gave to me—a brothers' ring—flies high, symbolizing thanks and admiration for all he ever did for me. Today, indeed, was for him, and he, of course, provided inspiration from above as I set a new PR: 3:26:17, shattering my previous PR by 14 minutes, 57 seconds! We're dancing.

My Grieving Process

It would be more than two years after this marathon that I would run another marathon that helped me to mature further intellectually in my grieving journey. The site of the marathon this time was Oklahoma City, which had tragedy of its own to deal with after the bombings there. What I found was a city and community that had responded tremendously well and with such class to a tragedy that I was inspired and touched. I wrote another reflection and a letter to the race director to communicate what I learned.

Why We Run
The Oklahoma City Memorial Marathon—Sunday, April 28, 2013
(Written on the Eve of the Race)
It is the simplest of sports, really. Lace up the shoes—some even choose to go barefoot—and head out for a run. It's your heart, mind, and soul out there. That's all you have—how far will it take you?

For marathon runners, we strive for 26 miles, 385 yards. There is something special about that distance that demands you to dig deep and to see what you have in you. You draw upon memories of good times and loved ones, and the presence of the day itself to get you through.

The recent bombing at the Boston Marathon on April 15 was among the worst of terrorist attacks because it attacked the very spirit of marathoners and those who cheer on and celebrate that same spirit. The marathon is open to all, and the course has 52.4 miles of access (26.2 miles either side). Marathoners and fans celebrate freedom, inspiration, and the spirit for living.

I am reminded of a question my four-year-old daughter, Caitlin, asked me the day before the Boston Marathon. It was after Sunday school: "Why does God send people down from heaven if He's only going to take them back again?" Knowing loss quite well, having lost my dad and a brother far too young, I first said that it was a great question and that I don't have all the answers. I went on to say that, even though we end back up in heaven, it is great to have time on Earth to share with each other and to celebrate the journey together.

The Murder of Innocence

We have to try to enjoy the time we have together down here and make the most of it.

I think that is one element that is a part of all marathoners—making the most of it. It is far easier to stay under the covers on a chilly morning than to get up early to run 26.2 miles—oftentimes, the start and finish lines are at or near the same place. While we physically get back to where we started, we are richer for having lived the experience of a marathon.

Tomorrow morning, I will embark on my 33rd marathon and 29th state in my quest to complete a marathon in each of the 50 states. The site, ironically after the recent events in Boston, is the Oklahoma City Memorial Marathon, which commemorates the 168 lives lost here on April 19, 1995, to evil and cowardice. The city celebrates their lives and the lives of their loved ones who were forever impacted. Violence and evil haven't won. Freedom and good have outshone those losing forces by loving, inspiring, and showing courage.

When I lace up those shoes tomorrow morning and get to the start line, adjacent to the Oklahoma City National Memorial, I will honor the 168 who fell and the memory of my own loved ones, not only by beginning and completing the marathon, but also in the time I have left on my own journey.

Note I sent to the race director a couple days after the race:

Kari,

I just wanted to reach out to express my thanks for a true, first-class event. Before this weekend past, I had not been to Oklahoma and was not aware of The Oklahoma Standard. I am now richer for having experienced both. I have run 33 marathons (29 states), and yours is among the best.

The fact that you can't get a bib number below 169 is very powerful. The wall of the first 168 BIBs is humbling and very moving. It is a

My Grieving Process

perfect example of The Oklahoma Standard and how Oklahoma's resolve rises above tragedy.

I am sharing some thoughts [Why We Run] I wrote down the night before the race. Thank you for a great event!

Sam

I was surprised by what I learned in Oklahoma City, and it set me further on my course to find the right spirit to write this book. I was almost there.

For me, another important moment, being Michael's only younger sibling, was the day on which I would match his age at the time of his death: 39 years, 23 days—forever etched in my memory from seeing it the first time on his death certificate. That put the mark for me at March 30, 2014. With running being my primary outlet for stress relief, for talking and listening to my brother, and for grieving, I would find myself picking a marathon to run on that actual day and would write yet another reflection after having completed the race.

The New Frontier

Since my brother Michael's passing nearly four years ago, I have struggled with the fact that, as his only younger sibling, I was in the awkward spot of facing the day when I would reach his age (39 years, 23 days) when he passed away. That day was today, and being a student of the calendar, I decided to commemorate the occasion with the running of a marathon. The site: Reston, Virginia, for my 32nd state (36th marathon overall) in my quest to run a marathon in each of the 50 states.

This day and marathon have loomed for a few months. My left ankle has not quite been up to par, and I debated whether to postpone. However, sometimes, you have to cast doubts aside, roll the dice, and have faith that everything is going to be all right. So, I decided to go all in and make the journey to Virginia.

The weather forecast seemed to get worse and worse. By race-day morning, the outlook was 46°F for the start and getting colder, down to 40°F for the finish. Oh, and let's not forget about the relentless rain and 20–30 mph winds. While waiting to go to the start line, a gentleman I'd just met summed it up best: "These conditions are actually good. Going through hell has a way of making everything else seem easy."

The run begins. My feet are soaked less than a mile in. I actually thought about carrying an extra pair of socks to change into halfway through the race, but realized that would have been futile. I wonder most of the first half if I am going to take a step and have my left ankle remind me that maybe I shouldn't be out here. However, as I round the halfway mark, a comfort comes over me, and I sense that I have an angel on my shoulder to take me home. People often ask me why I run alone so much. I tell them that I never really run alone. I connect with those who have gone before me, think about the future, and rejuvenate myself for the present tasks at hand. Today was a perfect example of how I never run alone.

The second half of the marathon has it all, much like Michael. Rain gives way to calm for a few miles, and then the weather comes back with fury: sleet miles 18–21, snow the last several miles, and wind galore! Michael's spirit is alive, and he is having fun with me.

The course was designed mainly as a double loop of a half-marathon course. I missed it the first time by, but as I hit mile-marker 25, I look up and take note of the street number of the address at the start and finish line: 11400—in the European date convention, that's 11 April, Michael's birthday. He is surely smiling down. On to a strong finish and one more reminder of his presence: I finish in 4:47:28. That's 4-11 (4+7) as my sister, Frances, would later point out (sometimes I need a brick wall to fall on me). One last brick in that wall was when I got back into my car in Atlanta. I flipped the key, and the odometer read: 174011. No shit! Michael was born eleventh day of fourth month in (19)71 (reading odometer backwards).

My Grieving Process

A day and a run that I will remember and draw upon forever! Here's to you, Michael! Thanks for always being an inspiration and propelling me onward.

I still believe in a higher power and that the spirits of those we love so dearly have a way of surrounding us. What I lost faith in—and still have no faith in—are the leaders in the catholic church. They possess neither the understanding nor the desire to correct the situation of child sex abuse for the better. For that reason, I no longer attend a catholic church or follow any organized religion.

After this race, it started to settle in that I did not know what was next, and I did not know what was holding me back in writing the book. I will explore that more fully in the next chapter, "Breaking My Own Silence," but it was not until a very reflective weekend and several months and years of battling through my own depression and anxiety that I decided to go "All In" and finally publish this book:

Are You All In?
January 29–31, 2015
Arizona, U.S.

I had registered for the Sedona Marathon and had planned to run it on Saturday, January 31. A buddy of mine, Ray, and I flew into Las Vegas on Thursday—cheaper to fly into Las Vegas than it was into Phoenix due to Super Bowl weekend there this year. We made the 4½-hour drive to Sedona from Las Vegas on Thursday, stopping by the Hoover Dam to enjoy the sights and to see the completed Mike O'Callaghan-Pat Tillman Memorial Bridge, a beautiful arch and concrete-steel composite bridge standing 840 feet above the Colorado River and 1,500 feet downstream from the Hoover Dam.

Friday morning, we took in the sights and magic of the red rock colors in Sedona as much as the rain and fog would allow. At 11 AM

MT, we headed to packet pickup for the marathon. There, the race director informed us that the marathon had been canceled. The Forest Service deemed a section of the course unsafe due to the rain (blah blah blah . . .). Upon my suggesting other options to the race director, it became clear he was a can't-doer:

"Sorry, there's nothing we can do."

"Sorry, you can't do the half-marathon course twice. The police department won't support that."

"Sorry, you can't get a refund. We are going to give you a $15 credit toward next year's marathon." The race fee was $90 . . . gee, thanks for the generosity, Mr. Race Director!

I took my can-do attitude, got on my iPhone, and started to search for other nearby marathons. I found the Yuma Territorial Marathon in Somerton, Arizona, also planned for Saturday morning. I called the marathon office there, explained my situation, and they gladly welcomed me to come down. So, we packed it up and drove another 4½ hours to the southwest corner of the state near the border with Mexico.

It turned out to be a very pretty drive, and we found that Yuma is a beautiful part of the country. It has miles of lettuce, lemon trees, and other produce. It is considered the winter lettuce capital of the world. Blue skies, flatlands with rich, black soil, and bright-green lettuce growing in abundance in between mountains in the distance and the surrounding fields; fresh air and plenty of sunshine combine to make an awesome landscape. What a beautiful place we would not have otherwise had the chance to see!

The race course was simple out-and-back and flat. It had beauty all around. The bigness of the sky and openness of the land inspires a broader view of life and who you are. I took in the positive energy.

My brother, Michael, always has a way of saying, "Hi," during my marathons, so it seems. This race, I was not really looking for a sign. With a little more than two miles left in the race, the most beautiful

My Grieving Process

white seagull flew into my view from out of nowhere. It stopped just off to my right without crossing the road and then flew back off to the right in the distance. It was as if it got my attention just to say, "Hi." A few seconds later, it became clear who was saying, "Hi": Good old #11. The mile-marker sign for those running the half marathon showed they had just completed 11 miles (for me, I had completed 24.1, with 2.1 still to go). This mile-marker sign was the only one that I had seen turned horizontal during the race so I took extra note of it. Michael's birthday is April 11, and since the release of white doves after Michael's funeral in 2010, I have always found extra meaning and inspiration in the presence of white birds flying overhead when I see them.

This marathon was a lesson in the power of will and re-dedicating myself to my goal. I could have used the Sedona Marathon cancellation as an excuse not to run this weekend and maybe even second-guess my long-term goal. Instead, I found a way to check off another state in my quest to run a marathon in all 50 states. When life throws you a curve ball, you can hit the long ball. Where there's a will, there's a way. I'm all in.

Many people wish to win the lottery, and I have sometimes, too. In short, though, I no longer wish to win the lottery—because I realize that I've already won it in that Michael was my brother. I would not feel moved to write another marathon reflection regarding my grieving and understanding with respect to Michael's passing until fall 2018, and that reflection is as follows:

> *Life is a balance of holding on and letting go.*
> *— Rumi*

Race-day Rush
October 7, 2018
Newport, Rhode Island

Arrival in Boston on Thursday, October 4, brings back memories: Logan International Airport is the first airport at which I landed after my first flight in 1991 (Pittsburgh to Boston). That trip had my mom; brother, Michael; sister, Anna; and me all along: I was heading to Phillips Academy, inspired by Michael, for a summer session before my junior year of high school. That was 27 years ago.

On this flight, I have my son, Luke, and daughter, Caitlin, by my side—ages 13 and 10, respectively. They are lighthearted and having fun with the start of fall break and looking forward to vacationing and fun times ahead with cousins in Boston and seeing Rhode Island for the first time. Symbolic of the youngest generation within our extended families, they are blissful, happy, and carefree. They are excited for the snack cart to come by to see what special treats they can get: Pringles for Luke and pink lemonade—in celebration of Breast Cancer Awareness month—for Caitlin. (My wife, Lynne, had to fly up a day earlier for a funeral. Her uncle, Pete, age 77, passed away from pancreatic cancer, and his death is the first in her mom's siblings' generation, as that generation has a much closer view of the sun setting on them.)

Arrival in Newport on Friday, October 5, conjures up feelings of anger and longing. Michael is no longer here. I miss him. Being along the beautiful New England coast this time of year reminds me of where Michael cheered me on in 1998 for the Cape Cod Marathon in Falmouth, Massachusetts. I can still hear him saying, "Come on, Sam! Bring it!" as he rode his bike alongside me the last several miles of that race. He had a way of inspiring, driving, and enabling me to reach for new heights and frontiers. He was the best—not only my "Best Man" in my wedding party but also my best man throughout his life, and he was only four years older than I, blazing new paths himself as he lived. I was gunning to finish in under four hours. Cheered on by Michael,

My Grieving Process

I crossed the marathon finish line at 3:57:31, a 9:04-mile pace. That was 20 years ago.

More than eight years have passed since Michael's tragic death in May 2010, and more than ten years have passed since his first suicide attempt in June 2008. Much has changed. I miss Michael; that part hasn't. Nobody and nothing will replace him. Much of my anger stems from how Michael died, and I have to remind myself sometimes to focus more on how he lived. Died how? Too tragically. Died when? Too soon.

Next comes race-day morning. I decide to walk from the hotel to the start line, about a mile away. I approach Easton Beach in Newport. What has to be a couple hundred or more seagulls are along the beach. Another minute or so goes by before they all take off into the sky together. They take flight. It's a beautiful sight. It's the start of race-day rush. I feel Michael's presence—I feel closest to him along the coast and when seagulls are present. We had doves at the end of his funeral, and his ashes were spread into the Mediterranean Sea on a cool September morning in 2010, with seagulls flying overhead. Some of him literally remains in the seas while I hope much more of his spirit remains with me.

At the start line, a couple of the starter's comments ring true. First, stairs—as in staircases—are not welcomed by any marathoner the day after a marathon, including professional marathoners (she cites a quote by one). Second, marathons involve pain, and that we all have to visit the pain closet from time to time. We don't necessarily enjoy the pain, but working through it shows our strength and makes us stronger. Why else would we run 26.2 miles to finish in the same parking lot from which we started several hours before? In my 48 previous marathon starts, I don't recall a starter hitting upon these messages, and her comments ring true.

That subject of pain is a tricky one for me. I lost my dad at age six. That involved pain. Losing Michael has involved much pain. That pain doesn't go away. I have to accept it. I have to sit with it. I have to be with it. I don't enjoy it, but there's not much else to do with the pain.

The solution is no solution—no need to try to dull the pain or look for ways to dull the pain. I can't forget it, but I don't want to dwell on it. No ruminating. With his death and how he was abused as a young, innocent child, I don't see any justice. Nothing will bring him back, but the perpetrators in no way have had to pay for what they've done. That's the no-justice peace. I have to sit with that—not be at peace with it, but to know and acknowledge that it exists. I still have to endure and deal with the aftershocks of pain that someone caused more than 35 years ago. Time doesn't heal all wounds. The passage of time actually seems to amplify how much I am dumbfounded, astonished, and maddened by all that has happened.

I'm 20 years older than I was in 1998—not quite as young, not quite as fast. For this marathon, I set the goal of breaking a 10:00-mile pace. I take the start slowly and steadily. I feel strong. My first half is measured, tempered, and reserved: 2:09:55, 9:55.0 per mile. I'm in position and on pace. The third quarter, seemingly always the toughest quarter of a marathon, I slow a little. As I head into the early 20s, though, I am inspired to bring it. I can hear, "Come on, Sam! Bring it!" It's go time. I pick it up, passing many other runners and attacking the hills in the final miles. The wind is at my back. I complete the second half: 2:08:46, 9:49.8 per mile. I brought it! Total time: 4:18:42, 9:52 per mile. It's my best time since October 17, 2015: Baltimore Marathon, 4:18:56, 9:53 per mile. I have become stronger since then, physically and mentally. I still miss Michael. I still have the pain. I embrace all feelings as I *be*—*just be*. I cross the finish line strong, honoring him with an arm and index finger pointed high into the sky—wishing he were still here and that the world had treated him better and that he didn't have to suffer. He was a truly beautiful soul in a too-often cruel and brutal world.

Time to focus on the future again and continuing to raise another generation that, hopefully, has less pain to process and accept—not *none*, just *less*. Hard to have one without the other, I suppose. As a line in Whitney Houston's "One Moment in Time" says, ". . . To taste the sweet, I face the pain. . ." As a line in Five for Fighting's "Chances" says,

My Grieving Process

". . . you gotta cry before you sing. . ." Pain has enlightened me, even though I haven't liked it—but, who does? Time to look again to the brighter sides of living—to stay on the sunny side of life, which helps to balance the pain. Good and bad coexist, as do feelings of depression and jubilation.

18

Breaking My Own Silence

*Look well into thyself; there is a source of great strength
which will always spring up if thou wilt always look.*
— Marcus Aurelius, Meditations

To break the silence about my brother through publishing a book like this, I needed to break the silence I kept myself—about what happened to me; about mom. I tried to push it down at times but finally worked through my own pain to be able to articulate and process the harsh realities of this story. While there were positive, loving moments and actions from my mother, they coexisted with a very negative undertone of fear (of her and God) and desire for perfectionism imprinted on her, as she was raised strictly in a catholic orphanage for the first seven years of her life. I finally reached out and began work with a therapist in November 2014, four-and-a-half years after Michael's death, to deal with my own pain and barriers. So, what was holding me back?

For starters, I was abused myself and never told anyone. My high school guidance counselor, Brother Clement Smith, tried to initiate a sexual relationship with me in the spring of my junior year. I would often stay after school and do my homework, waiting for my mom to pick me up after she finished work at around 5 PM. One day after school, Clement walked up behind me and pressed his erect penis, covered by his pants, into my right shoulder and armpit area. He put both of his hands on my shoulders and stood there for what seemed to be an eternity (in reality, probably about a minute). I was frozen. I didn't know how to react. I did nothing. I didn't say anything, but I think he sensed that I was not okay with it and that it was wrong. He never tried anything after that.

However, I never said anything. What would I say? Who would I tell? After all, Clement was the high school guidance counselor responsible for letters of recommendation to college. I wonder how many other boys he tried this with, and I wonder if he got further than he did with me. Maybe some of my classmates and other Pittsburgh Central Catholic alumni reading this book will now know that someone else was negatively impacted by Clement and will come forward. I know . . . Clement did a lot of good for many boys, but that does not make it okay to sexually molest and abuse boys! In fact, it is an even greater crime because he abused his position of authority and used the catholic cloak to hide behind, as did many others.

That was one thing that held me back. What was another? Being honest about my mother's own shortcomings was another one. She was another one who used seemingly loving deeds to hide behind other, outright hurtful, ones. She was verbally and physically abusive as a parent. I think her actions were impacted by her own rough childhood in a catholic orphanage until age seven and by a strict catholic upbringing in her adoptive family. There were a number of times that she abused Michael.

One day while we were playing Wiffle ball in the backyard, Michael did something to upset me. He was four years older and would often pick on me during a few-year period when he was around the age of ten. My mom exploded and chased him around the yard with a Wiffle ball bat, wanting to beat him. Michael ran under the camper in the neighbor's yard next door, the Andersons, and hid so that she could not swing openly on him. For about five minutes, she yelled at him to get out from under there. At the time, part of me was happy this was happening to Michael because he used to pick on me. In retrospect, I realize this was no way to treat Michael or any child. She eventually got Michael to come out from under the camper and proceeded to hit him several times on his rear end and the back of his legs, punishing him for what he had done. Parents, I ask you: Do you abuse your children? It is not okay to hurt your children. There are other ways to discipline and deal with your own anger.

Another instance of my mom abusing Michael was one Saturday morning when he was relentlessly calling me "Orca" (making fun of how fat I was as a child) and invading my space on a couch in the living room. My mom came in with a metal hanger and started to hit Michael. He ran upstairs to our bedroom as she proceeded to chase him, and he went under a bed. She took the hanger apart, straightened it out, started poking at him, and yelled at him to stop antagonizing me.

Another major instance of abuse I recall is when Michael was chased into my mom's bedroom and hit with a dust mop. I don't recall what he had done, but I do recall that he was hit and pressed hard enough into the wall that the drywall in my mother's bedroom cracked and collapsed between two studs. It was a hole that would go unrepaired for several years until my brother Paul would help renovate her room.

My mom verbally abused my other siblings. When my brother Paul was growing up, she would yell at him, "Be a man! Get out of this house. Live on your own. What kind of a man are you?"

Paul lived at home until he was 30 years old. He didn't go to college; he worked as an engineering draftsman at a local steel plant. With my mom not in the business of helping her children to plan for college—Michael would be the first to break the mold—Paul found himself in that awkward spot of trying to leave home but not knowing how to. My mom's love was abusive toward him. Instead of constructively helping him to chart a course to leave home, she berated him and questioned what kind of man he was. She also demanded, in an emotionally abusive tone, that he pay rent to live at home. Yes, paying rent teaches one responsibility, but when it comes to yelling at your son hurtfully, that is not the way to do it.

My sister Anna dated a black man in her 20s. Michael was still at home, going to high school, and Anna was living at home. My mom did not approve of her dating a black man. One night, Anna came home, presumably from seeing LaMonte. My mom erupted, questioning her to see if she had been out with him. The argument escalated and resulted in my mom saying several times over, "You're nothing but a good-for-nothing f*#king ni~~er-lover!"

My sister Frances was more on the promiscuous side and explored her sexuality as any young adult might. For anyone who was raised in a strict catholic environment, sex is bad and not something to be talked about. One summer, when I was in high school and Frances was still living at home, she had been going out on dates with several different guys. One night when she came home late—after curfew—my mom was irate. She proceeded to question her on what she had been doing and concluded by saying, "You are nothing but a scum whore slut."

In some ways, I was my mom's golden boy or her "angel." I was largely seemingly protected from outright assaults. However, she did hurt me, too. The most hurtful things I can recall my mom doing directly to me physically when I was a child are washing my mouth out with dish soap when I swore and smacking my hands with a wooden spoon when I would do something bad. The most hurtful thing my mom ever did mentally to me, though, was when my acceptance letter for a summer program in architecture at Cornell University between my junior and senior years of high school arrived in the mail. I'd been accepted! I was in. This would be an awesome program—one that Michael had inspired me to attend, and it would allow me the opportunity to build a portfolio, which I would need to be accepted into the architecture program as an undergraduate. Due to our family qualifying for maximum financial aid, we would have to contribute only a small portion (about $500, as

I recall) toward the cost of the summer program. When my mom got that letter in her hands, she tore it up! She was upset that Michael had instigated this and that he was encouraging me to seek out opportunities that she thought were "out of our league." She would always yell that, and it still echoes in my mind sometimes to this day when I am seeking out new opportunities. Instead of encouraging us to grow and develop, she wanted us to remain under her domain. She always wondered why her own children, namely Michael and me, did not want to stay closer to home and take care of her. I was outraged and upset. I went up to my room, pounding up the stairs and crying, yelling that I hated her. Of course, I came around, I guess, and came to terms with it—that I had to accept it because she was the only parent I had—and I moved on. I did not, really—until I processed that moment fully in a therapy session some 22 years after the fact. That was one of the major hurdles to overcome in writing the book—still loving my mother, being thankful for the positive things she did but acknowledging that she had major faults and engaged in behaviors that contributed to the abuse that my brother suffered.

In deciding to publish this book, I had to come to grips with everything involved. It was not only the poor leadership in the catholic church but also the broader impact of a culture created by a catholic church upbringing, poor aspects of my mom's parenting methods (and her own refusal to seek the help of a mental-health professional to deal with her own demons), and society's general misunderstanding of how to help people in conditions such as Michael's. Was I going to put everything on the table, as I have done, or was I going to single out the catholic church and leave it at that?

The choice was rather easy for a number of reasons. The truth sets you free—as it has done with me. I also assumed the catholic church would likely attack this book, our family, and anything else to undermine our credibility. It does not want to make the difficult decision of admitting it is wrong and realizing that it cannot ever adequately care for victims' needs because its primary aim is to protect itself and the pedophiles who operate within its institution. I am presenting the full picture of factors in the hope that everyone sees the truth and draws their own conclusions. The leadership in the catholic church is not without fault, parents are not without fault, and society is not without fault. What are you going to do to help change things for the better?

How do we stop the cycle of abuse? By *reviewing the truth* so that we do not blindly duplicate negative behaviors in the future for our own children. By summer 2014, I had seen that I had become very angry, depressed, and anxious over everything going on in my mind regarding my upbringing and Michael's pain. I saw myself overreacting and being angry with my own children, duplicating some of the same bad behaviors (e.g., yelling) that I had witnessed. I decided that enough was enough and that I had to get help myself. I reached out to a therapist, something that, while I was growing up, I was told represented weakness: "Why would you need to talk to someone? Why would you go to a perfect stranger and reveal your thoughts?" For those of us who have already seen therapists and sought professional help in times of need, we know the strength and courage that represents. For those of you who have a negative view of psychiatry and psychology, I ask, "Why?" Would you not go to a cardiologist if you had a heart problem? Would you not tell your loved ones that you had a heart problem? With mental illness, it's different in most cases, but it does not have to be. We should be able to say, for example, "Look, I have major depressive disorder and general anxiety disorder. I am working with a good therapist and need your support." It sounds odd, I know. However, we will have made progress when it does not sound odd and when those with mental illness can talk freely about their mental-health challenges, just as many others can talk about other illnesses and ailments.

To this day, it seems that my siblings and I have had to be the parent for my mom. Being an orphan, it was as if she looked to *us* to parent *her* since she did not have her own parents. We had to do things that a parent would or should normally do. Michael and I had to fill out our own applications for financial aid. Michael had to show her around college campuses, as opposed to her showing us campuses and inspiring us to grow beyond her nest. To this day, she looks to me and her other children for emotional support and to take care of her. This remains a frustrating aspect of my mom's personality and behavior. I know it wore on Michael.

For example, when my mom would visit him in New York City, he had to greet her at the airport and take her back to the airport. On one visit, when my mom was headed to the airport to head back home to Pittsburgh, Michael erupted and insisted that she take a taxi by herself to the airport. He would hail the cab for her, but she would ride alone. She refused, cried, and ended up convincing one of Michael's friends to take her to the airport in the cab. It is indicative of a much larger emotional burden that Michael carried, along with my other siblings and me: At times, we had to parent our mother.

19

My Sister Frances's Thoughts on Our Dad, the church, and Michael

After Michael's death, each member of my immediate family reacted differently. Still today, we each talk about it differently. Over the years, Frances has shared some of her thoughts in heartfelt emails. What follows are excerpts from those emails that provide further insight into our family situation, my dad's perspective, and Frances's own perspective regarding Michael.

Frances's email to me, March 1, 2012

> If Dad had lived longer, he would have been a wonderful influence on you, at least from everything that I remember. He was a very kind man. He was funny and fun to be around. Even when he yelled, or after he threw things when he was mad, two minutes later, he'd sit down and talk with you and tell you that he loved you.

The Murder of Innocence

As I get older, I certainly realize the stress parents are under trying to manage the household, working to provide for the family, and having energy left to play. Dad always took time out to play. I know you were very young when Daddy died, but he did love spending time with you. I remember seeing you and him rolling around the living-room floor wrestling and tickling each other. I remember him holding you and being very proud of you.

Dad used to take us to the movies or roller-skating rink, or to get ice cream. We would all pile into his Ford Torino, and off we'd go. We went to the drive-in a lot. I also remember trips to McDonald's and taking long drives. Sometimes he would take the long way to Grandma's house. (Note: Grandma was our paternal grandmother.) Do you remember that? We would say, "Hey, Dad, take the long way," and he would.

We would sing, "Over the river and through the woods to grandmother's house we go." It sounds real goofy now, but we did do that.

I know things were tight with money, but I never felt like I was missing anything. Dad and Mom made sure we were always clean and had "nice clothes" to wear. There were times as I got a little older that I might have asked for things that weren't within the parameters of our family budget, but I didn't really care if I didn't get everything I asked for. I later found out that I had received exactly what I needed.

For example, on one occasion Dad and I had gone shopping at Sears for clothes. Of course, I wanted Jordache jeans! They were the rave back then. Those jeans were $40. Yes, that's how much they were, and Dad said, "No way!" So, he picked out a pair of Jordan jeans. Yes, the name of the jeans was Jordan! So, of course, we got the Jordan. They looked just like Jordache, and the design was even better. I'm not just saying this. The Jordan even fit better, too! They were about $15.

Dad did reassure me that it didn't matter whose name was on my jeans. I was beautiful, no matter what. I had great confidence because of the way he spoke to me. Even though I was disappointed

My Sister Frances's Thoughts on Our Dad, the church, and Michael

that I didn't get the jeans I wanted, I understood what he meant. We had fun shopping that night. Dad always stopped at the snack counter at Sears on the way out. My favorite was the large, salted, warm cashews. Yummy!

Of course, the day came when I needed to wear my new jeans to school (of course, only on certain Fridays, when it was jeans day). So, I wore them. Everybody loved them! I looked good in them, and I felt good, too. And I thought, *Look, no one cares what name is on the pocket.* That is, until, Mary Smith and I were in the bathroom, and she looked at me and said, "Hey, those aren't Jordache. They're Jordan! You don't have designer jeans." (Of course, she's the only one who noticed.) Now, this situation could have gone one of two ways. I could have become upset and cried or been ashamed, but Dad didn't raise me to respond that way.

So, I looked her straight in the eye and said, "I know. I don't care. My dad bought me these jeans, and I love them!" I walked away proud and confident. Nothing was ever said about the name of my jeans again. That is the kind of dad our dad was. I know you are that way as well with your children. Dad always taught me to be proud of who I am and where I come from. He would tell me all the time that family comes first. No friendship comes before family. Always stick up for your siblings. If they are in trouble, help them. Make sure you're always there for each other, and never let anyone speak ill of any member of your family.

One day at church—yes, at church—Uncle David decided to come to a morning mass during the school week. Uncle David came to church that day with men's boots, but they had a large heel. Also, it did look as if he had light-blue eyeshadow on, and he did have some mascara. Yes, it could be considered by some to be quite embarrassing. But, once again, I remembered what Dad said. *Don't ever be ashamed of your family or where you come from.* I remember Uncle David seeing me and waving, and I waved back and smiled. So, after mass, some of the kids asked me who that was. I said, very confidently, "That's my Uncle David." Some of the kids asked why he had girls' boots on, and you could tell they weren't being very nice. All I said was, "I guess he likes his boots," and I left it at that.

I remember feeling comfortable. I remember not worrying. And you know what, Sam? I wasn't embarrassed. I was happy about the way I reacted. And, I noticed at that moment that Dad was right. If I'm not embarrassed, and if I'm comfortable with who I am, then people should have nothing to say. It's the insecurities of others that people feed on. After mass, I did go over and give Uncle David a hug and a kiss, and I didn't worry about a thing.

I thought I had one of the best childhoods ever until Dad died. I was the one who told Michael about Dad. I was so afraid that evening. I remember Anna waking up, yelling, and asking why everyone was in the house. Initially, I just told her to be quiet. Then, I did wonder what the heck was going on. I didn't know why Grandma was in our bedroom; she wasn't at our house when we had gone to bed. Grandma looked at me, touched my face, and said, "Something happened to your dad."

So, I did what any catholic Italian kids would do. My knees hit the floor, and I prayed. I begged God to make my daddy okay. I prayed and prayed. I remember asking God to take me. Just give me one more day with my dad, and I will go instead. I'm not just saying this. That's exactly what I did. I knew that God would never take my dad. God is the one who keeps us safe.

After Anna had spent herself yelling so much, Grandma told us the truth. Dad was gone. I didn't believe her. I went into the hallway and stood at the top of the steps, listening to sounds and words that I didn't understand.

Then, the boys' bedroom door opened, and there stood Michael. He was rubbing his eyes from the hall light and asked what was going on. I said to Michael, "You have to go back to bed."

"Why?" he said.

And I just blurted it out, "Because Daddy died."

He looked shocked. I told him not to tell anyone that I told him, because I didn't want to get in trouble. Keep in mind that I was

My Sister Frances's Thoughts on Our Dad, the church, and Michael

only 12. Paul woke up, too, and Michael and I told him what had happened; he just turned around and went back to bed.

I don't remember what happened next. I do remember being at the dining-room table a little later that night, and Mom walked through the door. She was inconsolable. I didn't understand, at that point, what she must have been going through. The next person I remember is, well, he [Richard J. Dorsch] is the man who would come to hurt Michael. I guess that's what people did back then—call a priest when someone dies. Dorsch was in our house. I didn't understand the significance of his presence until many years later. (I guess the grooming of our family had begun.) I do remember that he grabbed Mom and slapped her across her face. I was afraid. I didn't know what to do. As I said earlier, Mom was totally inconsolable, and I guess he did that to try to get her to stop screaming. Nonetheless, in retrospect, it seems quite abusive and inappropriate. Why would Mom have tolerated that or have continued to be in touch with someone like that?

I know Mom did the best she could to raise us. Her love for us was never in question. What I struggle with is her blind faith in the church and how she never thought to question anyone in the church. I am angry about the way some catholics are taught and raised, which is to trust clergy and not to question anyone in authority. They tend not to question a priest or a person in a leadership position. Why do they trust totally in someone just because that person claims to represent God? As soon as God's name is thrown into the mix, they assume purity and goodness must follow. What a bunch of shit!

I know Mom believes that her faith got her through the loss of Dad, but that faith made our family vulnerable. That faith put us in the most dangerous place of all, church.

What's really sad is that, still today, many catholics are terrified to speak out against anyone in the church. How sick is that? How can that be? It's outrageous to have children and not question why an adult male (priest) or an adult female (nun) wants to be alone with your child(ren).

The Murder of Innocence

I remember Michael saying that he expected more outrage from Mom when he told her about the abuse. At first, I didn't understand his comment about outrage. I now understand what Michael wanted from a parent. No matter how hard it was for Mom, she needed to give Michael the support he needed. I'm not saying that she wasn't upset or devastated, but she needed to take the responsibility because she was supposed to be his protector, the guardian of his innocence. It was on her watch that Michael was hurt.

I don't know why some parents don't take responsibility. It doesn't mean they wanted it to happen—it just means that they need to reflect on their actions and find where they fell short. And then, let the injured child know that they fell short and that this never should have happened. The child needs the adult to bear the burden of the guilt. This is what is so sick about this type of crime. Not only does the child not know what's happening, but also, the child ends up carrying the guilt almost all the time. The guilt must be taken from the child. It is too much for a child to carry, even as they grow up and become an adult.

I know you were very young when you lost Dad, and I need you to know that he did not have blind faith. Daddy read the bible—which so many catholics don't do! Why read the bible when you are taught to rely on the pope and priests to interpret for and preach to you? Dad believed in the power of goodness and virtue. He believed in respect and never compromising one's beliefs. He did not just follow what people told him to believe! Blind faith and trust are a very dangerous combination. Dad always told me never to go with strangers, and no matter what, go to him about anything. Anything at all! He also said that no one was ever to touch me or make me feel uncomfortable. Of course, I was only nine or ten when he told me this, so I wasn't sure exactly what he meant. All I know is that, if I ever felt that way, I knew I would go get my dad.

When Michael lost Dad, he was only nine years old. I don't know if Dad had a chance to tell Michael about those types of dangers. I don't know if Michael knew to go tell Dad. Did Mom

My Sister Frances's Thoughts on Our Dad, the church, and Michael

ever talk to Michael about strangers or anyone ever touching him inappropriately? Did Michael know to go get Mom and to tell her if he was uncomfortable?

If you look back, the signs were there. Michael would act out at school; he didn't go to school a couple of times; he hid in a garage one morning. He started acting out by throwing things and getting detention a lot. Oh, sure, one can say it was because Dad died.

But, did Mom or any other adult ask him what was really going on? Did they allow him the space and have the patience for him to feel comfortable telling the truth? Maybe Michael would've said something if he hadn't been taught to fear the church or to be ashamed of himself for sinning, even though the sin wasn't his. If Mom's blind faith wasn't clouding her emotional sight, maybe she would've noticed something.

What about the teachers who let Michael out of class to go over to the rectory during class time? What the hell was wrong with them! This is how blinding blind faith can be. What do you think a grown man wants from a little boy during class time in a one-on-one setting?

I remember one day when I was on the back porch when Michael came home. He got out of the car, ran to the side door, ran right up the steps, and went straight to his room. Mom was in the kitchen. I went and asked Mom where Michael had been and with whom. She told me, "With Father Dorsch," and continued to clean the stove. She didn't go upstairs and check on Michael; she just went about her day. I didn't understand this.

I remember saying to her, "Why does he [Dorsch] always do stuff with the boys and not with us [Anna and me]?" I felt left out. Little did I know! Shouldn't that have been a sign to Mom—that, at first, he was taking all five of her children at one time, and then just her sons, and then just one son?

This is the problem with parents' or others' blind obedience to religious leaders. That blind obedience is often times passed onto the child, which is dangerous and unforgivable. A child should be protected, taught to think freely and critically, and encouraged to question authority. Too many people aren't intentional or thoughtful in how they think or live.

And, if you feel so strongly about a religion, for goodness sake, why don't you participate in something? Why would you just go sit in a pew week after week, year after year, and do nothing within that community? What can you possibly get from that? If you want to talk to God, you can talk to him anywhere—you don't have to sit in church around a bunch of people who are there just for the sake of being seen.

When I got in trouble at school, Dad would want to understand both sides of the story. For example, I smacked Sister Nancy in the face on one occasion. Not on purpose. I was standing in the lunch line, and suddenly, everyone pushed really hard. I was not expecting it, and I flew forward and fell right into Sister Nancy. She grabbed me and smacked me, but I didn't realize who'd hit me because it happened so fast. So, I just hit back. Natural response, right? So, after about ten seconds, I realized what had happened. I was the only one who got in trouble. Off to the office I went, and Dad and Mom got the call.

Dad and I went to the convent that night to discuss what happened. To say the least, Sister Nancy was angry. She demanded an apology and wanted me to be punished. Well, then Dad spoke. Calmly and respectfully, he asked for all the details of what had gone on. He listened and then asked who else was in trouble and how other kids had been reprimanded. He also asked if the other kids had apologized for pushing me. She told him that no one had apologized to me and that no one else was in trouble. Sam, I sat there thinking: *What is this? Dad is standing up for me?* Dad told me to get up and that we were leaving. He told Sister Nancy that I would not be apologizing to her unless she had an apology for me. *What?* I thought: *This is awesome!*

She would not apologize, so we left. As we were leaving, she said that she would pray for us. Dad looked at her and shouted, "No! We'll pray for *you*." At that point, he explained to me that, even though I had hit her, it was an accident and that I should

My Sister Frances's Thoughts on Our Dad, the church, and Michael

not have been singled out like that. He spoke up. He stood up for what he believed in and how he felt. I wish you could have had the chance to know him more. I wish every day I could have known him more. Yes, he yelled, and, at times, we got hit, but there was often a lesson to be learned.

Speaking to your children—as I know you already do—will stay with them forever. I remember talking to Michael on the phone one morning while Douglas and Madison were in preschool. This was right after his first suicide attempt. I was still trying hard to comprehend what had taken place just months earlier. And, as we spoke, I thanked him for sharing his story and for being alive. I told him on the phone that day that I would be a better parent because of him. I would listen to my children. I would give them a voice, and I would make them aware of dangers. That's what I told Michael. My children know what a pedophile is, and they know to tell me—and to tell everyone, to shout it from the rooftops.

I sit and wonder today why Michael didn't know of these dangers. I question why Dad was taken before we had knowledge about our dangers. Blind faith and blind obedience to others are the most dangerous behaviors in this world. How can you give someone that much power over you? Why don't people question things? Because it's so easy to let someone else think for you. So, at what price comes this blind faith? The price is immeasurable, as we have found out. It costs children their innocence, their souls, and even their lives. Why do I see this now? I was so focused on Michael getting better that I didn't see all the pain. Also, I struggled with the fact that I never saw Michael as a victim. How can this absolutely handsome, well-educated, self-confident, easygoing—and yes, sometimes, quite-pompous man—be a victim of any sort? I didn't know, and therefore, I didn't see.

I remember being at Bellevue Hospital in New York. It was when Michael was leaving there to go to Sheppard Pratt. I had arrived that morning with some breakfast and pastries for Michael. I had brought him his computer and phone charger. I remember that morning so vividly. He looked amazing. Even though he was on a psychiatric floor and in a blue hospital gown, he looked better than anyone in the entire hospital. He was fit, his complexion was flawless—his eyes a piercing blue. He stood tall as he spoke to the physicians and made his demands. He was not bending or compromising for anything or anybody. I remember that he was extremely annoyed that morning. I had spent more than 90 minutes on the phone with United Healthcare and with the diocese. I tried to reassure and comfort him—and he looked at me like I was crazy. (And, of course, now, I understand.)

He yelled at me and said, "You just don't get it, do you? You don't understand! They took my life—my *life!* I will never know who I was supposed to be!"

I was shocked. I didn't understand. I didn't take it personally. I knew he was upset, and I was there to help. My response was, "Well, you can be anything you want to be now. You can do whatever you want with your life. It's your choice."

He looked at me and said, "You just don't get it."

And he was right. I didn't get it. I thought *Well, okay, you're upset. I know things happened, but you can get past this.* I had always believed that, no matter what, as long as you chose the right direction, you'd make it. I believe in goodness. I truly believe that good triumphs over evil. No matter what, taking the higher road will lead to better things. Michael always lived his life that way. He always chose such a beautiful path.

I believe you must forgive to go forward. You do not forget, nor do you accept, but you must let go of a past you cannot change. Unfortunately, the past would not let go of Michael. I believe he tried as hard as anyone would ever fight. As I meet other survivors of this unforgivable crime, I notice they all struggle with the grip that the past holds. They try to shake it, but it will not leave. It shows up for no reason—it doesn't matter what time of day or night, or if they are at work or with their children. Nothing stops this intrusive pain.

So, what is one to do? I also feel it now. I have been betrayed. Someone my family trusted hurt my brother right under my nose.

My Sister Frances's Thoughts on Our Dad, the church, and Michael

I didn't notice. I didn't know what sick, disgusting things my younger brother was being forced to do. This man sat beside me at dinner in our home. Every day I realize what this sick individual took from me and my family. And now, I get it. It doesn't go away, and you don't ever forget.

So, now I must find a way to show the world what happens when you have blind obedience to authority. We as a society must make sure that no child ever experiences this type of crime. It is the only way to prevent losing them. Laws and attitudes must change. Knowledge and awareness are the only defense. If I get angry, I can't focus on the good, and the bad will eat me alive. So, I promised Michael that I would stop to listen and find out how to help. I would always give him a voice. I know he needs all of us to give him a voice. My voice must have knowledge, wisdom, respect, and dignity to represent such a remarkable man.

This type of betrayal is exhausting. It leaves you feeling exposed, stupid, vulnerable, and questioning "Why?" all the time. I can see how those who experience this firsthand get very tired. For us to live through it secondhand is overwhelming and devastating, as well.

I feel betrayed when I reflect back on my memories. Once Michael experienced betrayal, he should have been able to come to us. We should have had a chance to protect him sooner and right after the first incident. I think of all the times I was with him as a child, adolescent, a young adult, and even reaching middle age. Through all those stages of life, we talked, laughed, shared stories, and often just hung out together. But I never knew what he was going through. It does bother me sometimes that his close friends knew more than I did. Why couldn't I help? Why didn't he want me to know? Why didn't he tell?

We need to teach our children to *tell*. We need to teach our children to be logical thinkers. Know when to question, and never be afraid to question. I strive to reach this goal with my own children, and in time, with children throughout the world by speaking out about what happened. If our children are hurt, we hold the responsibility. It is our job and society's job to keep children safe—to give them a voice.

This email is getting long, so I'll wrap it up. I just want you to know I am aware of all that was taken from you. Daddy didn't live long enough for you to know him, and Michael, who was your #1 role model and best friend, died far too soon under tragic circumstances.

I know we all must find a path that will lead us where Michael will be safely remembered and never forgotten. I know we will do great things with Michael's foundation. I can't wait to see all the good that will come from this. We are already winning in the sense that Michael had the courage to speak out before he left us. And, the world is listening. The trial in Philadelphia is just the beginning. Ten years ago, the media would not have even covered this issue. Journalists, media, teachers, doctors, lawyers, and parents know that we need to do something, and they are starting to talk. I am not afraid to speak out. Michael started the path, and we will finish it.

Frances's letter to me, February 15, 2015

I am feeling very overwhelmed today. Once again, I find myself wishing I'd been brought up in a completely different environment, one that allowed for free thought, curiosity, and positivity. The more I reflect on how we were never allowed to question anything or anyone, especially a priest, the angrier I become.

I can't believe that anyone is comfortable teaching an innocent child that he or she is born a sinner. What type of thinking is this? In our case, we (innocent children) were taught this by a pedophile and men and women who protected such pedophiles. Sometimes I find myself getting very frustrated that Mom didn't question these leaders, but she never would have questioned them because that's how catholicism works and how she was raised. Mom was raised in a catholic orphanage until she was seven years old, and all she remembers is fear. She was terrified of the nuns. She remembers having her ponytails cut off. Who the hell does that to a child who has no other adult in the world to protect them?

My Sister Frances's Thoughts on Our Dad, the church, and Michael

Then, she was adopted. For an adult to say, "I am in debt to my parents for adopting me," and, "I owe them for adopting me," makes absolutely no sense to a sound mind. She was a child, helpless, with no adult to protect her, and she never defended her thoughts or pursued her own path in life. She just listened to whatever she was told and never questioned it. It doesn't make it right! It doesn't mean we have to tolerate that kind of thinking, but you do have to take that into consideration when you are writing about her reactions and comments.

The problem (this is my viewpoint only) is that Mom was never allowed to speak her mind, and she never learned how to think for herself. I don't know why, as an adult, she did not break that cycle. I'm guessing that she had fear beaten into her so much as a child that she couldn't overcome that deep fear as an adult. There was too much to reconcile mentally. Why did the institution that *saved* her life also do so much evil?

Mom is a poster child for what is wrong with teaching religion so absolutely to young children. You destroy their logical thinking, you hinder the mind from questioning, and you teach blind obedience and tolerance of evil, which is dangerous and totally unacceptable. All religion involves power over someone else's mind.

The sad thing is that fearful little girls and boys grow up to be fearful adults with children, and the church takes full advantage of this mentality.

The primary blame sits with leaders in the catholic church, including the pope and everyone who knew about abuse and covered it up. How can you possibly hold a leadership position in the church, whether a priest, nun, bishop, cardinal, or pope, say you believe in some higher being, and then rape or cover up the rape of a child?

Parishioners, including Mom and Dad, played a part, too, because they fell for the church's deception and didn't adequately protect their children from the wolves dressed in sheep's clothing. Dad might have questioned more than Mom did, but he still allowed us to be raised catholic. I can't help but think that if Mom and Dad would have been raised differently, then maybe this never would have happened to Michael. Surely, if Michael hadn't been raised catholic the way he was, this wouldn't have happened. But it happened, and it's still happening to other children and families today.

I want to somehow undo what's been done. The "what if" question opens one's eyes to many possibilities for a different result. Imagine: What if pedophiles were reported to the police the moment abuse occurred? What if that would have happened in Michael's case? Would he still be here today? If any victim before Michael (sadly, we know there were other boys Dorsch abused before Michael) would have been encouraged to take the right approach and report the abuser, it's possible that Michael's abuse may not have happened at all.

I've tried to get parishioners to listen. Try standing outside of a church with signs about abuse. That's always fun. The worst reactions come from the church elders and the women who are 50 and older. They don't want to hear a thing. They are dead set on buying an insurance policy into heaven. I bet if the priest or bishop lit a child on fire in front of them, they would still defend the actions of the priest! It's brainwashing! It's amazing. I can't even imagine having that kind of power over anyone.

Even when Mom and I went down to Saint Paul's Cathedral in Oakland (a neighborhood of Pittsburgh) to hold signs with Michael's name Mom asked me, "Are we were going to get in trouble?" Seriously? A grown woman worrying about "getting in trouble"? It's just one more measure of the complete control the church has over people's minds—for life. Why in the world would we be in trouble for speaking out?!

Now, transfer that power to the developing mind of a child, a child who is repeatedly told never to question the authority of a priest. Imagine the man you were taught to idolize, the man you were taught to respect—because he's the image and likeness of God—rapes you shortly after your dad dies. You've just been raped by your God. No one can even imagine the betrayal and the negation of every developmental stage the child has managed to come

My Sister Frances's Thoughts on Our Dad, the church, and Michael

through—only to be damaged and altered forever when the person you were taught to idolize abuses you. How is a child to cope?

I'm still uncovering different layers from speaking to victims—how the abuse affects their marriages, relationships, identity, trust issues, relationships with their kids, work, family, alone time, sleep, intimacy, sexual orientation, etc. How can they be expected to live with such a heavy burden while the predator is free?

I'm really happy that you are writing. I have so many post-it notes, loose-leaf papers, and scraps of paper with feelings and emotions on them all scattered about. I find that, when I start writing, my emotions go into overload mode. I felt that, if I could just write my feelings down, I would feel better. It's not working for me like that just yet. I think writing confirms that it happened. If it happened, I have to accept it, and I just can't seem to do that. I can't let him go. I can't say goodbye. I can't accept what happened.

I am not embarrassed to say that I spent last Monday on the phone with a crisis representative for 90 minutes because I was having an especially bad day. Hey, that's what they're there for, right?

I want to respond to your comment about what we could have done better.

I think about the events that took place in our lives daily. I am in disbelief that it is coming up on five years that we were forever changed. I keep thinking, *What could I have done? Why didn't I do this? Why didn't I say that? Why didn't I understand more?*

There are times I wish I had more time to absorb exactly what happened to Michael during his childhood while he was still with us.

I think about how long it must have taken Michael to understand exactly what had happened. As he grew, he learned about the effects slowly; it forever changed him as he began to process it. We didn't have that kind of time to process it. We knew how horrific it was, but we could have never known all the complex effects of the abuse that he had to deal with. At least not at that moment. We were focused on the recovery. *What do we do now? Where is he going for treatment? How long does treatment take?* You focus on that moment. *What's next? How can I help?*

When we all learned of the news, it didn't sink in. Not right away, not instantly. Not for me, it didn't. You're not able to absorb all the effects. That's what I struggle with. I feel like now, each day, I understand a tiny bit more.

I wanted to help as much as I could. But there's the key word: *help*. How do you help someone when you don't even understand all of their pain and experiences? Oh, I *thought* I understood. I truly *thought* I was helping. I *thought* that, if we talked about it, if he knew I supported him, if we were all there and we loved him, we could make this situation tolerable. I believed that there is nothing you can't survive as long as you are willing to fight.

Well, in my mind, Michael's fight began sometime in his thirties. How dumb was I to think that? I didn't understand his full struggle. For some reason, my mind was not letting me absorb all of that because I never saw him struggle. Sometimes people say you have to lose something to truly understand the full effects. I don't believe that is true. I believe that, if we'd had more time, we would have been given a chance to understand better.

Dealing with Michael's loss, I find myself thinking: Is this how Michael struggled daily? The overload of emotions from losing him throws my body into such a state of shock and pain. Is this the way he felt dealing with his loss of innocence? I never expected grief or pain to hurt so intensely, to the point that you think you may die. That is the way Michael's absence is affecting me. And I know we are all grieving, each in our own ways. Is this how Post Traumatic Stress Disorder affects you daily?

How can some people survive such horrific events in their lives and others not come out of it? I remind myself that Michael was a survivor, and he survived better than most people ever do. He did come out of it with a wonderful respect for life—with a desire to constantly improve and the ability to connect with others on such a remarkable level. What a great life he created for himself! I'm so happy that he made all of his decisions about who he would become and where and how he'd live his life.

My Sister Frances's Thoughts on Our Dad, the church, and Michael

Sometimes I smile and think about how he'd order whatever he wanted to eat—no matter the restaurant or if the price was listed or not. That's funny! I would always say, "I'm not going to another restaurant with you unless the prices are listed!" Who's the crazy one? Me! I really can smile when I think of those aspects of his life. He *did survive*—and with great force and determination. Michael made strides to improve. He rose to the challenges of life and succeeded way beyond even most who *have* no such burdens to carry. This is a true lesson learned for those of us who don't take the time to seize the moment. (You are certainly not included in that statement!)

It's funny that you mentioned Dr. Ross today. He was the one I called quite a few times after what happened. I remember going into such a hysterical reaction when he told me what a "tormented" young man Michael was. I remember feeling such anger. I thought, *Who the hell is this guy to be telling me my brother is "tormented"? I would know if my own brother was tormented.*

He went on to say that he meant Michael had a lot of issues that needed to be resolved. That still didn't help, because I was mad that I didn't know all the issues. How can I know my brother my whole life and not understand what he was going through? This alone is a struggle for me to accept. I wish I'd known more; maybe I could have helped more.

You know what's really amazing? When Michael was at Sheppard Pratt and Austen Riggs, I would call him to check on things and to make sure everything was going okay. I would actually get off the phone in a better mood than when I called. *He* actually made *me* feel better. How is that possible? It's true, though. And, we would always laugh. I don't remember a phone call or conversation with Michael when we didn't laugh.

Anyway, I just felt like sharing today. I think that, since Valentine's Day is just around the corner, I'm feeling a bit overwhelmed. The last note that I sent Michael was a valentine. My mother-in-law was here, watching the kids, and I had her, the kids, and me make Valentine's Day cards, and we mailed them to Michael. Mine was this cheesy little card that I wrote in. I wrote: "Roses are red/violets are blue/I am so lucky/to have a brother like you!" And then I put in a little smiley face.

I know he received the cards because he called to thank us. I also remember being at Mom's house when she received Michael's belongings from Austen Riggs. In the box was my valentine. I couldn't even touch it. I left it with the other items that Mom has at her house. It just did something to me to see that in there. I experienced a feeling of disbelief—the overwhelming feeling that this is way too big of a loss to handle.

At this point, there is still no way for me to truly comprehend the loss. It comes in little steps. Just as I'm sure Michael learned of how the abuse affected him during his steps in life, I, too, will learn the effects of the loss step by step. I don't like these steps, and I don't like feeling the impact. It's a blow each and every step of the way. I guess I have to learn how to process the blows. Some days—as you know—they really knock you out.

Take care.
Love You!
Fran

My Sister Frances's Thoughts on Our Dad, the church, and Michael

Michael holding Frances's son, Douglas, shortly after his birth. Michael loved the innocence and promise he saw in his nephews and nieces.

20

What I Would Have Done Differently

I received a call in the early hours of Saturday morning, June 21, 2008. It was Michael's now ex-boyfriend telling me that he'd found Michael unconscious in his bathroom and had him rushed to the hospital. I would fly up later that same day with my brother Paul to see Michael. We would be there the following day when Michael woke up from his overdose.

I spent a few days in New York with Michael. Paul ended up staying longer. I had to get back to Atlanta because my daughter was expected to be born within the next few weeks. The last time I saw Michael on that trip, I told him that I loved him. But then, I added as I was leaving, "The next time you think about doing something like this, you'd better call first."

I was mad at him for attempting suicide. Looking back on that, it's ridiculous. I was upset at someone in so much pain that he wanted to die. I didn't realize how much help Michael needed. In the months that would come, I would fight for him and work to get him help, but there was still much of me that wanted him to be there for me, to be the big brother who always looked out for and guided me. I was not used to having to care for him.

When I speak of some of the paradigm shifts that we all need to make as a society when we have loved ones battling with mental illness and pain, I am speaking largely to the fact that we need to accept that they might not be able to play the role for us that they once did. That shift in what they can do can happen very quickly and leave us with very little time to process and transition to that new state, but I believe that's one of the things we *must* do to drive better outcomes in the future.

Didn't fully get where he was . . .

Or, I did, but I didn't want to accept it. During his second suicide attempt, one of the things he threw out the window was a commemorative frame with pictures of us, race numbers (bibs), and finisher medals that I had framed along with the poem I had written to capture our day running the New York City Marathon on November 7, 2004. I was mad that he threw it out the window. While that was a natural reaction, I did not fully accept that, for him to have done that, he must have been really, really sick.

One regret I have is that another thing he gave away was his brothers' ring. After his first suicide attempt, Michael bought himself, Paul, and me each a Tiffany Atlas ring that we dubbed "brothers' rings." Michael was so touched that Paul and I flew immediately to New York upon learning of his first suicide attempt to be there with him when he woke up. We all then agreed that we would not be having any more suicide attempts as we started to wear the rings. Michael later told me, during fall 2009, that he put his ring in a random tip jar somewhere in a Starbucks in Manhattan. The thought crossed my mind to buy him a replacement ring for Christmas 2009, the last Christmas he would come to share with us, but I did not. Part of me was mad that I even would have to do this—he broke his own promise that he made in buying and gifting the rings. Part of me also thought, *Was it my way of not locking him*

What I Would Have Done Differently

down again with the ring—meaning making him stay? After all, he was in so much pain, and I did not want him to have to feel obligated to me. He had come to know many obligations and must-do's throughout his life. All that said, in retrospect, I would have bought the ring.

Part Six

Loose Ends

21

For the Common Good

This chapter is meant to reply to some of the common responses or challenges I get when I share Michael's story and as I strive to bring about change.

The first major argument is that the catholic church does more good than harm—this is what I call, "The for-the-common-good argument."

Sorry that this horrible set of circumstances happened to your brother, but the catholic church does more good than harm, so you need to move on. You should not be attacking the church.

To be clear, I am not attacking all churchgoers. I am simply trying to hold accountable the bad leaders in the catholic church who committed wrongs against my brother and the many other bad leaders in the catholic church who have abused other children. The pope and the senior leaders in the catholic church need to take action against their own bad leaders instead of protecting them and responding inadequately to the victims of those bad leaders' abuse. The church leaders too often try to turn it into an attack on the church. It should not be an all-or-nothing proposition. The church is not all wrong or right; they just have not adequately addressed the issue. Is the fact that Michael's abuser, Dorsch, spent less than a month in jail for all his crimes *justice*?

Another argument that I get is that we are all sinners. *Dorsch sinned, but you are a sinner, too.*

Someone once emailed me back, ". . . I don't pray for God's justice, which would condemn everybody. I count on His forgiveness, which can save everybody." This email was from someone who thought I should not write this book. I should just move on. *God will save us all.* That is the complacent and passive tone that too many church leaders want. It is another one of their traps—*just pray to God for change and trust us; nothing needs to change.*

All organizations have problems. You are just bitter at the catholic church because they directly impacted your brother negatively. My own wife sent me the following note:

> ". . . Just last week there was an article about a sex predator working at an FCS (Fulton County School) elementary school. Yes, child sex abuse exists in our school system, and this is not the first time. The former Crabapple Middle School/Milton High principal who caused three DUI accidents earlier this year? Guess what? He got a slap on the wrist and is still employed by FCS. Remember when Luke was in first grade and an MPE (Mountain Park Elementary) teacher got fired for bringing drug paraphernalia to school? I'm guessing she got moved elsewhere. Remember last year when a child got bit by two charging dogs in aftercare after school on the MPE playground? Scary people exist outside of the Catholic Church."

She was still advocating that our children attend Sunday school regularly at a catholic church. She and her family had a positive experience with a priest, and she tends to be on the side of accepting that bad can happen anywhere. That may be true, but that doesn't mean you allow it to happen and don't fight for change. The catholic church could be in a better spot than it is today if it would simply respond to child sex abuse victims adequately and stop defending itself as righteous at all costs.

22

What Survivors of Child Sex Abuse Want

What do child sex abuse survivors want as they aim to move forward positively in life? Several months before Michael died, he wrote a poem called, "A Tree in Stockbridge." It articulates what child sex abuse survivors want:

A Tree in Stockbridge
Down on Main Street
Past the Daily Bread café
Where locals and tourists meet,
A Canadian maple is halfway
In shedding leaf upon leaf.
I stand in my belief.
There is a place for me
When the season will change

And I can just be,
Unturned,
Again, as upon a free range,
The person I choose,
Returned,
With nothing to lose.

The poem hits at the heart of what child sex abuse survivors want: Simply to be what they would have been had the abuse not occurred. Michael often said that his abuser stole his life from him. It is the catholic church's moral—and should be legal—obligation to give survivors whatever they deem necessary to get better. That varies by victim. The catholic church should not be seeking to cap any financial obligation to the victims while they are perpetually funding the perpetrators—even long after those criminals are convicted.

The catholic church should fund a totally independent, third-party, arm's-length organization to administer and oversee the care of child sex abuse survivors who are still working to overcome the abuse they withstood at the hands of the catholic church. The church itself is in no position to care for child sex abuse survivors directly, as its main aim is to protect its own interests and the perpetrators within its own walls.

Child sex abuse survivors also want statutes of limitations lifted. Our family was not able to sue the catholic church and Dorsch for the original crime. We had to rely on the argument that the catholic church, once it started paying for Michael's mental healthcare, could not withdraw unilaterally as it wanted to do and did. Ultimately, the courts ruled that the catholic church did not make things worse, as Michael had already tried to commit suicide in June 2008, when payments started. That, of course, is exactly wrong, as the catholic church and Dorsch started making things much worse for Michael back in 1981, but the laws prevented us from going back to the original crime in court. If you live in a state such as Pennsylvania, which has such statutes of limitations, please work to get those lifted so that justice can be served.

Life insurance and disability benefits

If Michael had died on his first suicide attempt, he would have had a life-insurance-plan payout from his current employer at the time. Since he ultimately lost his job, he ended up with no life insurance (you should always keep it separate from your employer, by the way, and own it outright). Life insurance is for survivors.

If Michael could have gone on short-term or long-term disability before the full-blown, downward spiral, he would have had a better chance at the stability of income and a continued employer. Instead, he lost his job because this wasn't done soon enough, and he had a stigma around him at his then employer after his first suicide attempt, which eroded their confidence in him. I think we as a society underestimate the power and challenge of mental illness. If we tell someone we have cancer, they get it and can understand why we need time off. If we say, "Look, I am struggling with C-PTSD, major depressive disorder, whatever else . . . ," the response is generally not one of understanding, and, in turn, those battling those mental illnesses do not feel comfortable getting the help they need. It becomes a Catch 22.

Survivors' admitting they need help and how to treat them

Going back through my brother's files, I came across a medical assessment performed at Austen Riggs that describes his state of mind. It was performed October 16, 2009, a few months after his second suicide attempt:

> *. . . He also reported that July 2009 was the anniversary [technically, first suicide attempt was night of June 20, 2008] of last year's suicide attempt, with an OD on Ambien in 2008. He said at this time that the suicide attempt was a major blow to his sense of independence, and he hated relying on others and felt "shortchanged" and that others were "selling me short" by not allowing him to have space to run his life and always thinking he would kill himself and that his judgment could not be trusted. He viewed this 2009 increase in depression, "avoiding reality," isolating, and the fight with his*

landlord as evidence he could not make it on his own and that he was a "failure." This thought is what he said prompted his decision to go out on the ledge [of his apartment during the second suicide attempt in July 2009]. He says both of his suicide attempts were impulsive, and he has never really planned to kill himself and thought of ways to carry it out. It seems like usually his depression and flashbacks occur along with psychotic thinking or "detachment from reality" and that psychosis doesn't occur independently.

It may be that his desire not to be a failure and to be trusted has a lot to do with why he doesn't want to be on medication, even given the long-term risks he faces. He is aware of these risks, and he understands that both depression and psychosis could occur again in the future and might impair his ability to use his own judgment in getting help if they did occur.

This last paragraph is especially impactful for me. I wonder how much my brother did not want to use medicine to help him because, growing up, we were told that you did not necessarily need psychiatry or psychology to help you, in the rare times such subjects even came up. It is okay to use medicine if mental-healthcare professionals think benefits outweigh the risks. Even while my brother was in and out of mental-healthcare facilities, my mother was skeptical that they were actually helping him. I actually think he would have died even sooner if he'd had no treatment at all. Seeking out help is a good thing.

For those of you helping loved ones battling mental illness, you have to help them consider—with the help of their doctor—if medicine might help them. Refusing it out of outdated notions or ridiculous stigmas of psychiatry and psychology does not constitute a good decision, and the result can be a deadly spiral.

23

It's Worth Living

Life is like riding a bicycle.
To keep your balance, you must keep moving.
— *Albert Einstein*

Early on in my journey after Michael's death, when I was just beginning to realize how hard it was to move forward from the pain, I wrote the following. As I re-engaged with writing this book in June 2014, I came across it and thought it might be helpful to anyone going through pain and trauma.

It's Worth Living
Sam Unglo, June 27, 2010
What does it all mean? It's a question that is worth asking. There is so much that happens in life such as pain, tragedy, and suffering that begs the question, "Why bother living at all?"

But therein is the magic—for it is in living positively that we outshine the darkness. Think of all the greatness that exists in inspiring someone to achieve more, loving them, helping them to become something they never thought possible. Love is the answer.

One's goals in life should include the following:

Becoming the best I can be. The challenge is to be disciplined and not to be distracted by or overindulge in the pleasures of this world. It's about *balance*: working hard, enjoying, playing, finding time to set goals, and advancing the ball forward for your family, friends, and society, working for the common good.

Facing obstacles head on. When you need help with something, ask the people who love and care about you for help. You can get through whatever the challenge may be. Do not resort to bad behaviors and bad habits to compensate for insecurity and anxiety caused by challenges. The sun will always come up tomorrow, and you need to make a step toward the future each day—not try to complete the longer race all within the same day. Take comfort in knowing where you are, where you came from (the success you have achieved, thus far), and where you want to go.

Sharing wisdom. There are many out there looking for help and answers. If you find yourself wise about something others are not, share your wisdom with them. The peace that you help them achieve will, in turn, bring you peace.

Teaching others. It is in teaching that one truly masters his subject, whether it be academic, emotional, physical, or some other skill. Teaching others helps to elevate us all as humans.

Being a loving presence. Always respect and treat others with honor. Sometimes mean people need to be dealt with differently, but most people are genuinely good, and your kindness and caring toward them will pay dividends and lead to your own further advancement and opportunities.

Learning. Studying and learning are the keys to obtaining new knowledge and a better perspective on living. Always be reading and educating yourself to learn and become more. Open your eyes to new developments and opportunities.

Develop relationships. Invest in your professional and personal relationships. Don't view interactions between yourself and others as simply transactional. Take time to understand them. See how you can help them and share part of yourself to make them better as well as your overall relationship. There will be people you don't get along with, and that's okay, but again, most people can be understood if you take the time to listen and understand.

Be able to think from a distance. Read and reread *The Republic*. There are many great readings out there. The classics provide an interesting perspective on how the world is designed. Be conscious of how you think, what you want to change, and how to make progress within different systems, organizations, or networks.

Know yourself and your talents. Don't let people take advantage of you. Know what you have to give. Make sure you are treated fairly, always work in good faith, and honor the trust people put in you.

Believe in yourself. Be courageous. Go after things you truly want. Don't impose limits. You can do anything you want if you work hard, do your homework (always prepare and plan), and invest in making things happen.

24

Letter to Michael

I am standing on a seashore. A ship at my side spreads her white sails to the morning breeze and starts for the ocean blue. She is an object of beauty and strength, and I stand and watch her until, at length, she hangs like a speck of white cloud just where the sea and sky come down to meet each other. Then someone at my side says, "There—she is gone." Gone where? Gone from my sight—that's all. She's just as large in mast and hull and spar as she was when she left my side, and just as able to bear her load of living weights to its place of destination. Her diminished size is in me, not in her, and just at the moment when someone says, "There, she is gone," on that distant shore there are other eyes watching for her coming and other voices ready to take up the glad shout, "Here she comes," and such is dying.
— Henry Van Dyke

I miss you so much!
Tell me you are still there—smiling down with delight!
  What I wouldn't give to hug you one more time or to hear your laugh again—so many remember and miss your damn laugh—saying that it's okay and that we are all having fun!

I hear the brightness of youth and your abundant spirit in the splashes at Luke's and Caitlin's swim meets. I hear you often:

In the laughter of Luke and Caitlin as their innocence comes to life each day . . .

In the spirit of young children as they wave goodbye on the school bus each morning . . .

In the sweet smiles of babies just a few months old as they long to be held by others or in their mothers' arms . . .

In the winter skies that are blue and pure and possess a peace and calmness that are hard to find anywhere else . . .

In the middle of the hands held by parent and child that say, "I love you. I trust you." And that nothing wrong will ever come your way . . .

May your brilliant love protect us and keep us well. We will forever miss you and long for a time when we could share one more moment with you. Until we meet again, please keep the wind at our back, and shine your wisdom down upon us!

Love, your brother, your friend, who misses you so dearly—Sam

The deepest pain

Missing is the deepest pain. I have struggled with that hurt the most since I lost my best friend in Michael. There are events that I have wanted him to be here for. At the end of 2012, my wife and I moved into a larger house. It is a house that Michael would love, and he would be proud of me for having made such a wonderful home for my wife and family. What I have found, though, is that, no matter who comes over for the first time, including my own surviving family members, I am still angered by the fact that Michael is not here to share a meal or a drink with me in person, and I am left longing for his presence. The way in which he died, the injustice done to him by Dorsch and the church, and the fact that I get to see him no longer all combine to make me very sad. It is from that very pain and sadness that I draw upon to speak out so that others can avoid what Michael, my family, and I have had to go through.

Letter to Michael

A great friend to many

An email that one of Michael's friends sent me on the one-year anniversary of his death highlights Michael's awesomeness as a friend. It shows his inner beauty.

> **TO: Samuel J. Unglo; Fran Samber**
> **FROM: Alli Schwartz**
> **SENT: Wednesday, May 4, 2011, 11:34:44 AM**
> **SUBJECT: Thinking of You**
>
> Hi, Sam and Fran,
>
> Just wanted to let you know that I am thinking of you and your families today. I still cannot believe Michael is gone and truly cannot believe it has been a year. Not a day has gone by without me thinking about him.
>
> I'm not sure if Michael ever shared this, but on 9/10/01, Michael and I had dinner together downtown. We left the restaurant, and I remember Michael looking up at the lighted World Trade Center and marveling at their size. The next day, 9/11, my husband was in the towers when they were hit. He barely escaped. Needless to say, it was a very emotional time for us and everyone else. Every day after, Michael traveled all the way downtown to meet me for lunch to be with me. Every day for three months! I never asked, but it was clear: he was trying to be there for me through a very hard emotional time. This was a very significant time in our lives together. It was significant for everyone, but for us, it changed our friendship. It added a different, deeper level that could not be replicated by everyday happenings. We had been through a very traumatic time together and pulled each other through it.
>
> After we got ourselves together, Michael and I organized a two-person parade (he and I), to help re-elect Rudy Giuliani as mayor for a third term. We put together posters, attached them to broomsticks, and marched around the city—across midtown, then down through Chelsea, ending up at ground zero. We would chant, *"Rudy,*

Rudy." Our parade was small, but it brought us years of laughter. People were honking horns in support, and some were yelling at us that Rudy sucked. We didn't care—we had fun and really believed in Rudy and how he handled 9/11.

I bring this up because on Sunday early evening, for the first time, I begged, begged Michael for a sign out loud (like a crazy person), a real one, one that he knows I will get. A sign that he can hear me when I talk to him in my head or when I think of him or when his family thinks of him. "Just let me know you can hear us," was all I kept saying.

It was Sunday night when I heard about the death of Osama bin Laden. Okay, I'm not totally off my rocker—it was bound to happen, but the timing of the event brought significance to me. It was the night I begged for a "real" sign and the week of the anniversary of his death. And I know that, if Michael is going to give a sign, he will go all out :). So, I take comfort in that.

Whether that translates to you or not, it's okay. But I did always want to share the 9/11 story with you. Meeting me for lunch every day, downtown in SOHO, just a few blocks from Ground Zero. That's who he was. I miss him, and I miss having someone to call and say, "Remember when . . ."

I hope my stories brought a smile to your face today and gave you comfort in knowing that his memory will forever be carried on through the foundation and the people's lives that have been touched.

All my love,
Alli

Letter to Michael

On depression

The following is a poem my paternal grandfather wrote to my paternal grandmother, presumably while he was stationed in the military, away from her. She struggled with her own depression at times throughout her life, and I love this poem for others of us who struggle with depression.

Smilin' Kid

By Michael Martin Unglo
February 4, 1930—Hidalgo, Texas

Smile!
   The world is blue enough
   Without you feeling blue.
Smile.
   There's not half joy enough
   Unless you're happy, too.
Smile.
   The fruit trees are always blooming
   And there's plenty fruit to pick, too.
Smile.
   This world may not be heaven,
   But then it's home to me and you.

25

Resources

Massachusetts Society for the Prevention of Cruelty to Children
www.mspcc.org
(Organization that Michael was very close to. We both raised money for them during our Boston Marathon 2009 fundraising efforts.)

Feeling Good—The New Mood Therapy
By Dr. David Burns
This is one of the first books I read as I tackled my own bouts with depression.

When Panic Attacks
By Dr. David Burns
This is another book by Dr. Burns that focuses more on preventing and controlling anxiety. I also found this one to be very helpful.

Steve Jobs' 2005 Stanford Commencement Address

https://www.youtube.com/watch?v=UF8uR6Z6KLc

This is one of my favorite speeches. Steve Jobs' main theme is that you can connect life's dots only by looking backward. In looking back myself, I see that writing this book has allowed me to connect many of my own dots (i.e., life experiences).

Maybe You Should Talk to Someone

By Lori Gottlieb

This is a great book for those of you who would like to see the benefit of therapy or to grow more yourself, even if you have already gone to therapy. Lori Gottlieb, a therapist herself, explores her own journey with therapy and provides case studies from her patients' experiences, in which you might find some similarities to yourself that allow you to see patterns you might otherwise not.

RAINN (Rape, Abuse & Incest National Network)

https://www.rainn.org

RAINN is the nation's largest anti-sexual violence organization. RAINN created and operates the National Sexual Assault Hotline (800-656-HOPE).

National Children's Advocacy Center

www.nationalcac.org

Their mission is: The NCAC models, promotes, and delivers excellence in child abuse response and prevention through service, education, and leadership.

Their site contains a wealth of resources, including the National Child Abuse Hotline: 1-800-4ACHILD (800-422-4453).

Resources

The Closing of the American Mind: How Higher Education Has Failed Democracy and Impoverished the Souls of Today's Students
By Allan Bloom

Michael had me read this book as I was starting high school in 1989. He always wanted me to think critically and to be a free thinker. This book explores those dimensions and looks at thought paradigms more broadly.

Dead Poets Society
Starring Robin Williams

Michael and I saw this movie together in 1989. It also entails thinking freely and being and becoming who you truly are. Robin Williams plays the role of a boarding school English teacher who inspires his students through his teaching of poetry. One philosophy for living that is shared throughout the movie is to "carpe diem" (seize the day).

The Michael R. Unglo Just Be Foundation
www.justbefoundation.org

This is Michael's foundation that I founded shortly after his death in 2010. You can learn more about his story and link to further resources.

26

Some of Michael's Other Writings

YARN

It's a thread called running
Stringing together three marathon victories
Across two continents and four years.

The thread runs in the family
From younger to older brother with
Me in the middle, having achieved the three.

The victories achieved were over a past self.
Of course, only one, New York, is a personal best,
Serving as bookends for the others, Atlanta and Rome.

✧ ✧ ✧

Master of Fine Arts Application—Literary Essay
By Michael Unglo, December 31, 2008

In the course of recovering from my suicide attempt, I have read many articles and a few books on health and wellness. One of the books is Carl Elliott's *Better Than Well: American Medicine Meets the American Dream*. I came across this book because of its specific references to Prozac, which I have been taking since being hospitalized in June of this year. Elliott has a lot of penetrating analyses of how we in America perceive ourselves and how our mental health intersects with our social institutions. His insights are especially relevant to my health status, and I share herein some critical commentary on the issues that he is addressing.

    A main tenet held by American medical professionals—both psychiatrists and psychologists—is that we the people have been obsessed with perfecting our personalities. In the pursuit of perfection, we are stricken by any number of mental-health conditions: generalized anxiety disorder, depression, and social phobia, to name but a few. Prior to the launch of selective serotonin reuptake inhibitors, people suffering from mental illnesses overwhelmingly limited their external expressions of self so as to control what the external world around them perceived of their intentions and wishes. In chapter 3, subtitled "The Face Behind the Mask," Elliott paraphrases from Christopher Lasch's *Culture of Narcissism*: "People became fearful of acting spontaneously or unself-consciously—imprisoned in self-awareness" (Elliott, p. 62, *Better Than Well*, 2004).

    On the eve of my suicide attempt, I had been attempting for several weeks to cycle off of the potent antidepressant Effexor XR, which had been prescribed by an internal medicine specialist, or internist. The reason for trying to taper off of this particular medicine had to do with unresolved depressive symptoms and profoundly disturbing flashbacks about my childhood and sexual abuse. A treating psychiatrist of mine has postulated that Effexor itself may have contributed to my suicidal ideation and actualization. Even though I willingly accepted my doctor's prescription for the Effexor XR starting in early autumn of 2007, I had expressed a general concern about the black box warning on my prescription. This warning, the most serious for prescription medications, had been modified and mandated by the Food and Drug Administration pursuant to a meeting of its expert Psychopharmacologic Drugs Advisory Committee on December 13, 2006 (Friedman RA, Leon AC. Expanding the black box—depression, antidepressants, and the risk of suicide. *New England Journal of Medicine.* 2007; 356:2343-2346). The Effexor XR black-box warning currently reads as follows:

> *Suicidality and Antidepressant Drugs. Antidepressants increased the risk compared to placebo of suicidal thinking and behavior (suicidality) in children, teens, and young adults. Depression and certain other psychiatric disorders are themselves associated with increases in the risk of suicide. Patients of all ages who are started on antidepressant therapy should be monitored appropriately and observed closely for clinical worsening, suicidality, or unusual changes in behavior. EFFEXOR XR® (venlafaxine HCl) is not approved for use in children and teens. (Accessed at http://www.effexorxr.com)*

Now that I am taking Prozac, to which I was switched while in the hospital recovering from my suicide attempt, I do feel like "the real me." The benefit of taking Prozac is that I am connected with living out my goals and dreaming up aspirations for my future. That is what I mean when I talk about "the real me," and the depression and Post-Traumatic Stress Disorder (PTSD), which have necessitated past use of other psychotropic medications, are in remission. I am also benefiting from ongoing talk therapy with an expert trauma therapist, who helps me with specific traumatic flashbacks that resulted in my development of what has been diagnosed as complex PTSD. Additionally, now I have a healthy libido and manageable sexual performance side effects, both of which can be compromised by any number of psychotropic agents.

In Elliott's chapter subtitled "The True Self," he quotes from the book *Listening to Prozac*: "This is who I am," said one patient after taking Prozac. "I just feel strong. I feel resilient. I feel confident."

(Peter D. Kramer, *Listening to Prozac* [London: Fourth Estate, 1994], 219). The ongoing debate as to whether these personal transformations in self-perception such as this patient's or that of mine over the past six months are chemically induced seems to me peripheral to the issue of healing. My goal is to connect with a present reality and future living free from the traumatic flashbacks that led me to almost take my life. Chemically enabled or transformed, my brain is feeling better as a consequence of taking Prozac. I think that Elliott hits the nail on the head when he writes the following:

> *Talk of the self permeates ethnographies, interviews, autobiographies, and memoirs. . . . The conceptual apparatus of identity has become a natural way of describing our psychopathologies, our ideals, and our aspirations. . . . Today, enhancement technologies are not just instruments for self-improvement, or even self-transformation—they are tools for working on the soul. (Elliott, pp. 52–53,* Better Than Well, *2004)*

Master of Fine Arts Application—Literary Essay
By Michael Unglo, January 13, 2009

I seek a seat in your fall class of graduate writing students, based on what I have read about your interdisciplinary approach to the craft. The goal is to develop further my storytelling skills that will help other people connect with the healing power of writing. I write to confront victimization, survival, and perseverance, all of which are relevant to anyone who is recovering. Of particular appeal as well is that your campus houses our nation's first Ph.D. program in Childhood Studies, and I would seek to complete my elective coursework by delving into that most important subject matter.

    The sad truth is that I was abused physically and sexually while growing up in Pittsburgh, and the hopeful fact is that I have connected with the nurturing power of education over the years. Essentially, my love of learning has been my saving grace in times past, and I wholeheartedly seek a seat in your program. Determined to escape and live free of fear and abuse, I turned to academics and became the first in my family to earn a college degree. Having achieved success as a copywriter in my first career working at advertising agencies in Boston, New York, and Philadelphia, I seek now to complete a Master of Fine Arts degree while writing a memoir. Indeed, I embark on learning the craft of creative nonfiction so as to help other survivors share their stories and connect with the healing power of the pen to overcome fear, shame, and guilt, to name but a few of the emotions to which abuse can hold us hostage.

At what point do cycles of abuse end? Conditioned from a young age to expect the worst, I attempted suicide on the night of June 20, 2008. The ripples of my attempt revealed the fact that my sexual abuser, the very priest who buried my father, had molested my older brother Paul before preying upon me as well. While on suicide watch at Saint Vincent's Hospital in Greenwich Village, I was hearing for the first time what we wished he could have told our mother three decades earlier. Her neglect of us in the aftermath of our father's death, by refusing to listen to "any more bad news," prevented Paul from protecting me. I see how cycles of abuse are byproducts of victims whose own lives devolve into transgressions, such as those committed serially by the pedophile priest who was convicted and jailed for the evil he spread around the Diocese of Pittsburgh during the 1970s through 1990s.

Since confronting the truths of my childhood and now continuing to heal from Post-Traumatic Stress Disorder, I support the work of advocacy groups whose shared mission is to prevent child abuse of all types. Currently I am in training to complete the 2009 Boston Marathon, which I am running on behalf of the Massachusetts Society for the Prevention of Cruelty to Children. In conclusion, I am reading Haruki Murakami's memoir, *What I Talk About When I Talk About Running,* which dovetails with my ongoing recovery as I work to assess honestly and openly what has gone right and wrong in my life. As I work on my memoir, which is the subject matter of my writing sample, I find my writing to be as much a part of my healing as my physical training for the marathoner's marathon.

My Better Manhattan Half

Michael upon completing a half-marathon in New York City, January 25, 2009
This is the ultimate moment for a runner: crossing the finish line. For me, this particular finish, at Bethesda Terrace on the 72nd Street transverse in Central Park, had seemed unattainable during the two months leading up to the race. Unemployed and recovering from a suicide attempt, I spent several hours each week in psychological counseling on the Upper West Side and keeping appointments with my psychiatrist on the Upper East Side. Just getting in the requisite physical training was a feat in itself. Finally, on January 25, 2009, I indulged in crossing the Manhattan Half-Marathon finish line with a self-congratulatory thumbs-up and ear-to-ear victory smile. A digital camera resting on a tripod at the finish captured this moment for me. Dressed in warm, yet lightweight, form-fitting tights, I braved single-digit wind chills alongside 5,000 other runners. The clock displayed a finish time of 1 hour and 41 minutes. I had logged a personal best, beating my past Manhattan Half-Marathon time by more than 16 minutes.

The race had started with my decision to resume running and get back into shape in the aftermath of my suicide attempt last June. Before then I had completed full marathons—three to be exact: New York, Georgia, and Rome. I ran those while trying to run figuratively from a past I wished had never happened. That past is the one that tripped me into a traumatic flashback the night I tried to take my life. The flashback itself was unleashed by a final quarrel with a lover at the end of a week when my mother projected her unresolved grief and depression onto me at the absence of her husband, my father, who had died some 27 years ago. While on suicide watch, a psychiatrist challenged me to consider running again someday, but to do so not out of a spirit of running *from* something. Instead, she encouraged that I run *for* something.

That is exactly why I was crossing the finish line in Central Park. This half-marathon was a victory for me en route to running for a cause in the upcoming Boston Marathon. Held in April every year, Boston is the marathon of marathons. I am dedicating my Boston Marathon to the Massachusetts Society for the Prevention of Cruelty to Children, an organization that was instrumental in bringing to justice the type of perpetrator who sexually abused me. I live with Post Traumatic Stress Disorder and depression because of the heinous crimes committed by a priest against me over the course of more than four years. Now that I run for the honor of all victims of abuse, these dozen-plus miles at a time—and a full 26-plus come April—seem like a walk in the park compared to the tolls exacted physically and emotionally by pedophiles.

Hands kept warm by Dri-Fit Nike running gloves and head protected from the winds by an Under-Armour Lycra hoodie, a digital camera captured the number—1709—pinned across my chest. Out of a field of 5,000 runners, I finished well under 1,000! This race demonstrated my renewed physical fitness and mental discipline. At one point, passing the upper reservoir and past the 102nd Street transverse where the Central Park Jogger was brutally raped and left for dead some two decades earlier, I recollected in a flash the time when, as a teenager, I was sodomized by my family's priest friend, who has since been defrocked and convicted for his crimes against other boys. These intrusions into present consciousness are endured by anyone who has suffered violence. Not all people find themselves haunted by flashbacks over the course of their lives, but for me, as I recover from a suicide attempt in which I sought to escape the hellish pain of a past event, experiencing such a flash on the road while running was not a surprise. Then I returned just as quickly to the road in front of me, before rising again to climb Harlem Hill at the northern end of the park abutting 110th Street. I drifted to good memories, too, as I recollected evenings watching Shakespeare-in-the-Park productions in the shadow of Belvedere Castle with friends.

My thumbs-up finish was a resounding answer to Hamlet's question. Having been blessed with a second chance to be, I have scored a victory for all survivors and victims of abuse.

Due West of Austen Riggs
By Michael Unglo, November 1, 2009

Spokes, more than a collection,
In fact, two wheels of them,
Sustained his reflection,
Maintained the bike's momentum.

Wind swept the rain against his face
Cold drops don't stain like warm tears.
He felt freer the faster the pace
And yielded no more to fears.

Across the turnpike overpasses
This state in which he connected
Briefly with no more trespasses,
Before a U-turn east to be dissected.

Bodies have minds all their own.
Does his mind feel his unique body?
His therapist listens to him bemoan,
But affirm he'll find peaceful remedy.

Not even 90 minutes had elapsed
Between departure from The Inn
And the time at which he collapsed
Onto a therapist's couch, Freudian.

27

Closing Thoughts

The following picture was taken when Michael was around eight years old, before the abuse would ensue. The caption in the paper read, "The youngster regularly makes waves at the Etna Borough swimming pool."

Michael, indeed, with the struggle he had to bear, made waves throughout his life. He spent his life in search of justice and how to move forward after his abuse. I encourage each of you to make waves in your own right. If we do not make waves, more innocent lives will be lost to this horrible crime. The perpetrators of this crime and their protectors count on silence to remain hidden. We have nothing to be ashamed of, and they have everything to be ashamed of.

Don't be silent. Be a powerful voice for the innocent, and keep speaking out!

The Murder of Innocence

Michael, before the abuse would ensue

Closing Thoughts

O Me! O Life!
By Walt Whitman

Oh me! Oh life! of the questions of these recurring,
Of the endless trains of the faithless, of cities fill'd with the foolish,
Of myself forever reproaching myself (for who more foolish than I, and who more faithless?)
Of eyes that vainly crave the light, of the objects mean, of the struggle ever renew'd,
Of the poor results of all, of the plodding and sordid crowds I see around me,
Of the empty and useless years of the rest, with the rest me intertwined,
The question, O me! so sad, recurring—What good amid these, O me, O life?

Answer.
That you are here—that life exists and identity,
That the powerful play goes on, and you may contribute a verse.

This book was Michael's verse. May his life inspire you to contribute your own verse, whether that be through:

Being a better, more understanding parent and a parent who advocates;

Being a better sibling who can support and understand your brother or sister;

Being a better pope or other catholic or religious leader who can bring about positive change and address victim and survivor needs completely;

Being a better legislator so that victims such as Michael can hold their perpetrators accountable for the original crime;

The Murder of Innocence

Being a better churchgoing member and community member by being on the lookout for pedophiles and holding all leaders accountable (remember: any good some people do does not allow them to do bad; you need to accept both realities and think);

Being a better friend and coworker to those suffering from mental illness;

And being a better whatever else you can think of to change this world for the better now knowing my brother's story.

Thank you for taking the time to learn more about the life of my wonderful brother, Michael. Just be.

Michael and me, December 2002

Michael at the Mausoleum of Hadrian, or Castel Sant'Angelo, in Rome, Italy

*Michael, October 10, 2009; finished 5K in 00:24:40
while on his journey at Sheppard Pratt*

"If you can't fly, run. If you can't run, walk. If you can't walk, crawl. But by all means, keep moving."
— *Martin Luther King, Jr.*

About the Author

Sam Unglo is the author of *The Murder of Innocence: The Truth about Sexual Abuse and the Catholic Church*. He is an honors graduate of Cornell University, an accomplished finance executive, keynote speaker, and the CFO of Boys & Girls Clubs of America. Sam has also devoted himself to honoring the life and memory of his brother Michael R. Unglo, who died tragically in 2010, and after which he founded the Just Be Foundation.  The foundation's mission is to end child sex abuse and to raise awareness and advocacy on behalf of child victims. An avid runner and multi-marathoner, Sam has completed 52 marathons covering 48 of the 50 states and at least one marathon per year since 1998. He lives in metro Atlanta with his wife and two children.

I hope that you were moved and changed by this book. Would you do me a favor please?

Like all authors, I rely on online reviews to encourage future sales. Your opinion matters. Would you please take a few moments now to share your assessment of my book on Amazon or any other book review website you prefer? Your opinion will help the book marketplace become more transparent and useful to all. Thank you.

www.ingramcontent.com/pod-product-compliance
Lightning Source LLC
Chambersburg PA
CBHW071226080526
44587CB00013BA/1513